THE PROGRESS
OF MUSIC

THE PROGRESS
OF MUSIC

By

GEORGE DYSON

'The singers go before, the minstrels follow after ;
in the midst are the damsels playing
with the timbrels.'

Essay Index Reprint Series

BOOKS FOR LIBRARIES PRESS
FREEPORT, NEW YORK

First Published 1932
Reprinted 1969

STANDARD BOOK NUMBER:
8369-1287-X

LIBRARY OF CONGRESS CATALOG CARD NUMBER:
79-93334

PRINTED IN THE UNITED STATES OF AMERICA

CONTENTS

'*WHOSOEVER is harmonically composed delights in harmony; which makes me much distrust the symmetry of those heads which declaim against all Church music. For myself, not only from my obedience, but my particular genius, I do delight in it: for even that vulgar and tavern-music, which makes one man merry, another mad, strikes in me a deep fit of devotion and a profound contemplation of the First Composer. There is something in it of divinity more than the ear discovers.*'

SIR THOMAS BROWNE : Religio Medici.

THE CHURCH

THE CHURCH

I

IN the centre of every European village there is a
church. In nearly every town that can claim a few
centuries of history, there is a cathedral. Scattered
throughout our lands, sometimes in fertile valleys,
sometimes in remote and forbidding wilds, are the
impressive remains of great monasteries, once the most
powerful communities, material as well as spiritual,
which our world could show. These legacies of brick
and stone, these columns and arches and towers, are
the most striking relics of our past. Seen through the
glass of history, they enshrine for us the major part of
what our ancestors meant by civilization, by corporate
devotion, and by the triumph of mind over matter.
They stand, solid masses of masonry, as permanent
memorials of the deepest and most persistent tendencies
in the chequered fabric of our common story. They
know no barriers of language. They have no political
frontiers. Wherever Western civilization has found a
lasting home, it has thus embodied its fundamental
creeds. These buildings are milestones, magnificently
impressive, along the road of man's spiritual pilgrimage.

Modern towns usually begin with a railway-station.
This is not quite so stark a contrast as might appear at
first sight. The railway now stands for that essential
communication between man and his fellows which is
the first bond of society. The road which preceded it
also had its stations, and more often than not they were
the village church, and the inn which proverbially
neighboured it. Thence came and went the pedlars,
the pack-horses, and the post-chaises which served our

forefathers as the railway serves us. Their stages were from one village green to another, or from a cathedral square to a chain of hamlets. Their time signal, when time mattered, was the church bell, the cathedral chime.

The church itself was very much more than a house of devotion. It was a meeting-place and a refuge. There the lieges could gather, or the outlaws find a hiding-place. It was put to many kinds of social use. It was often a granary and sometimes a stable. It was a stage, not only by reason of the sacred Act of the Mass there displayed to the people, but also by less exalted portrayal of homely themes and incidents, often more sacred in name than in method, which unfolded crude but vivid truths and stories to a people to whom seeing and hearing were the only avenues of thought. The church was a concert-hall, and not for the adornment of a musical liturgy only. It housed all those tentative experiments in descriptive anthem and oratorio from which so much of our music, secular as well as sacred, is descended. The church was a council-chamber for the guilds of merchants and craftsmen. Not rarely it was an open market where goods were displayed, bartered, bought, or sold. It would be a very narrow view of history that should account these myriad churches of our countryside to be exclusively religious in their by-gone use. Men were born, men married, and men died, and these elemental acts were given a communal significance and ceremonial long before common beliefs were formulated, long before any creed found a visible shrine. The Church ultimately took under its tutelage a host of customs and associations far older than itself. It then claimed, by adoption, a share in every corporate event which marked the lives of its children. Its children, in their turn, used the church for every social purpose. It was the one home of mankind in the mass. It was the one universal symbol of human brotherhood.

We have changed all this. We have sent our pedlars to the railway, our counsellors to the town hall, our merchants to their shops and markets, our millers to the elevator, our lenders and borrowers to the Stock Exchange, our actors to the theatre, our politicians to the club. That rich and varied pageant of all humanity which used to find its daily haunts within the walls or under the shadow of the church has not died. It lives and chaffers and gossips just as warmly and with just the same infinite variety as it did in the medieval church-porch. But it goes elsewhere. Our churches are lovingly cared for. They are far cleaner and quieter and more decorous than our ancestors would have deemed possible, or even desirable. We blush if we harbour a mundane thought in them. We tread slowly and silently and reverently. We make long journeys to admire their architecture, their stained glass, their monuments, their organs. We tremble to think what damage a profane hand or an ignorant taste might commit. Marvellously we protect, marvellously we restore. We preserve with meticulous care everything of historic or local significance; everything, that is, except the supreme historic fact that the church was once the unchallenged centre and meeting-place of the whole local community, busy men and idlers, rich and poor, old and young, traders, beggars, rogues, and lovers, men who worshipped and men who looked askance. Our consecrated gardens may now be trim, because the present world passes them by. Our cathedrals may be little more than the cherished museums of a life that is gone. A church can be very peaceful when it is empty.

There is loss as well as gain in all social changes.

The church of the Middle Ages was much more than a symbol of religious faith. It was a great social institution, and it remained the most important channel of social influence for just so long as it found room for all sorts and conditions of men, in their workaday thoughts and habits. When we build pews in our nave, and close our chancel, we may improve the comfort and decorum of our worshippers, but we destroy those easier manners of the past which allowed men to go in and stand a while, or talk a while, or kneel a while, at any hour and on any day, when either business or leisure found them at the church-door.

We are about to devote a few pages to that splendid heritage of music which comes to us from the Church of the Middle Ages. It would be a profound mistake to think of this music as the fruit of a peculiar sect. Medieval music, like medieval architecture, was an outpouring of the whole spirit of man. Cathedrals were not built by great ecclesiastics, however noble their powers of inspiration and resource. Cathedrals were built by master-masons, designed, elaborated, and erected stone by stone at the hands of gifted craftsmen. No spiritual fervour will of itself teach a man even the beginnings of an art. The music of the medieval church was written by musicians; by men, that is, of highly specialized technical gifts. Some were good men, some were bad men. Saints, knaves, and fools all had a hand in it. The Church could then find work for them all. Under no other conditions could an art so universal have been brought into being. For centuries Europe was amazingly rich in trained masons who were also great architects. She had also an inexhaustible supply of men so practised in music that no thoughts were too deep for its powers of expression. That all these gifts

were so generously devoted to the Church was due to
a relation of mutual understanding and respect. Artists
portrayed the high aspirations of religious communion
because the Church on her part provided a generous
home for art.

It has often been debated whether there is in truth
such a thing as religious art at all. There is good music
and bad music, just as there are religious emotions of
higher and lower order. These qualities can be combined in any degree. The scandalous masses written
around ribald popular tunes, which sometimes were
embarrassingly popular in the church, were often no
less talented, no less inspired, than those which more
carefully observed the proprieties. It is indeed doubtful
whether, without a long succession of such daring and
incongruous experiments, polyphonic music would ever
have reached its ultimate perfection of method. Nature
is prodigal of her gifts, but she is whimsical too, and
cares nothing for our nice classifications. We have to
hope that artists will be good men, or at least ready to
work within the accepted ethics of their time. We
demand so much of all men. But we do not expect a
good man to be on that account an artist. That would
be clearly absurd.

There have in fact been many of the great and good
who saw in all forms of art at best a snare, at worst a vice.
That has been one of the most persistent tenets of
puritanism in all ages. The old prophets who broke
down the carven images have found successors in every
age and clime. St. Jerome and St. Francis eschewed the
arts that they might not be distracted from a more
mystical devotion. Savonarola and the image-breakers
sought thereby to help men save their souls. There is
no limit to the length to which these negations can be

carried. There are religions where the very name of
God must not be uttered, lest the pure thought of Him
be in some measure narrowed or profaned. There are
sects where men's portraits, either in paint or stone, are
a sin, for God's image in man must not thus be counter-
feited. Every society draws its puritan line somewhere.
Some churches admit music, some do not. Some will
encourage voices, but find instruments unseemly. There
have been communities to whom the Campanile of
Giotto in Florence and the west front of Rheims Cathedral were vicious influences, to whom the nobility of
a spire, the beauty of an arch, the warmth of stained
glass, and the subtle smell of incense were alike ana-
thema. As for the grosser images of the heathen, there
are two approved lines of attack. One is to smash the
idols, the other to convert the idolater. It is of course far
easier to break a statue than to change a man's heart, but
both processes may be equally ignorant of artistic values.

And these restrictive sentiments may be as passionately defined and held among the devotees of a particular
art as among the iconoclasts outside it. To some people
music is rank emotion. It is a form of sentimental
suggestion only to be welcomed when it stirs the pulse
or melts the heart. If pulse or heart be of crude or
uneducated type, then music may become a frank
wallowing in primitive emotions. Others find such an
appeal and such a product unbearable. They ask that
the mind shall be engaged, as well as the heart; that the
decencies of restraint, the canons of form, the resources
of scholarship and craftsmanship shall not be over-
looked. They would rather have no music at all
than surrender their ideals of intelligent and conscious
discrimination. Such conflicts of attitude can be
traced throughout history, and can be plainly seen in

all societies, great or small, which use or abuse the possibilities latent in all the arts. And the two main contrasts, as between intellect and emotion, are often curiously mixed. A sect which is extremely hard and uncompromising in its creed may have wild outbursts of enthusiasm of the most emotional type. Individuals can behave no less inconsistently. A life physically athletic and practical is often fringed with emotional responses that are very near the surface and very difficult to control. The lower deck is proverbially sentimental. At the other end of the social scale are the nimrods of the countryside, who in their semi-artistic accomplishments can be relied on to take the predominantly emotional view. Men and women who in their daily pursuits would blush to show undue feeling, will exhibit a taste in music or pictures or literature which is in fact an emotional relief for the sentiments they repress in other spheres. It was our most stolid middle class which sang with such fervour the more emotional of Hymns Ancient and Modern.

We can study these problems with unusual clarity in the arts which the Church has fostered, because we have there not only a long perspective of history, but also a tradition still largely preserved and showing the main influences of that past. Just as her stones are so often a representation of events long gone, so her liturgy gives us a panorama of the spiritual and intellectual epochs in her thought. A chosen hour spent in an English cathedral can teach us social and musical history more vividly than any treatise on these subjects.

2

The very walk through the avenue which leads to the church-porch may revive in us that ancient instinct which found a peculiar sense of mystery and solemnity in the dim glades of a northern forest. Countless generations of men have there been moved to awe and worship, and it is no accident which makes those stone forests of Gothic architecture, columns and arches and aisles, appeal so deeply to our religious sense. Under a southern sun men copy in their temples the protecting shadows of a great rock. Gothic architecture reproduces the majestic shelter of great trees. So deep are these associations that our respective civilizations find it almost impossible to think of religious architecture in any other forms.

The plan of our cathedral is equally embedded in historic truth. Look through the west door and you will see in the very far distance that high altar where only the supremely initiated may serve. These ministers face the east, whence came their teachers and prophets, but whence came also that earliest glow of the sun which was a sacred beacon before history began. Not so far, but still distant, is the screen which divides the ordered hierarchy of office-bearers from the mass of common folk. This plan is not only religious history, it is social and political history too. Call it King, Lords, and Commons. Call it bishops, priests, and penitents. It is all one, a moving embodiment of just those divisions and just those loyalties which for a thousand years and more were the very foundations of our state. Later and more protestant faiths have expressed other views. There are modern places of religious worship where organ and choir are arranged like the orchestra of a concert-hall. The congregation occupies an amphitheatre of unbroken rows. The seats are upholstered and the whole building well lit, heated, and ventilated. The minister is not unlike a president, the first citizen of a republic, as it were, standing in his central rostrum in full view of the whole body of political equals who have chosen him. We build as we believe. We paint, we write, we sing as we believe. We can do no other.

Listen to the sounds which come rolling down the great spaces of our cathedral nave. Here too are vivid traces of the past. The poise and dignity of a chanted monotone, the inflexions and cadences which mark, by a fall of the voice, the close of a phrase or sentence; these are the very beginnings of music. When men crystallize their corporate thoughts into a form of words, these words very soon become, by constant association, so well known that they are taken for granted, yet so charged with feeling that alteration is unthinkable. This happens now precisely as it happened in the infancy of the Church. Even those Protestants who have stood most firmly against mere conformity in religious worship find themselves insensibly acquiring a very different practice, but in the long run a no less liturgical one. It is a matter of use and wont, associated with deep feeling. There is a story of a local preacher who shocked his hearers by the invocation: 'O Lord, roll your shirt-sleeves up!' He should have said: 'Lay bare Thine arm.' Every society which puts its thoughts and feelings into a form of words develops a sharp sense of peculiar fitness, in secular as well as in sacred phrase. There is an unmistakably ritual form in some of our lightest pastimes. One must not alter or invent a descriptive term, even in playing a game. And once such a form has been fixed for its purpose and occasion it is a small step to give it a still more exact and cere-monial character by chanting. Nothing is more uni-versal than this practice, in high and low civilizations alike. Repeat a significant word, and it becomes a cadence. A sentence becomes a chant, a chant a melody. To the stranger it may all sound like 'mumbo-jumbo'. To the initiate it is music. Hallowed by tradition and circumstance, it is sacred music.

When many voices chant together the words are lost, so far as clear articulation is concerned. Speech gradually changes into song. The practice of chanting the Psalms, universal in Western Christendom, could not have arisen except in communities intimately familiar with the words. A small choir may by careful practice chant so unanimously that the words can be spaced almost as naturally as in speech. But such singers are really singing from memory, for the hundredth time. It was thus that the psalmody gained so permanent a place in our religious music. The men who sat in the choirs of our abbeys and cathedrals a thousand years ago were going through an ordered sequence of religious offices day after day, month after month, year after year; and their predecessors had been chanting these same offices for hundreds of years before them. The Psalms themselves are of course far older than Christendom. It was the Jewish origin of Christianity which brought the Psalms so naturally into the Christian liturgy, and it is probably to them that we owe the initial power and place of music in the early Church. For the words did not come alone. Many of the most ancient church melodies must be attributed in origin to the still older Hebrew music of pre-Christian times. The subject of origins so remote is difficult and uncertain, but of the two sources mainly available, Greek and Hebrew, the internal evidence points definitely towards the Hebrew. There is no such warmth of tone and expression in the few fragments of Greek music which we have been able to decipher.

And in music of this elemental character, age and association are the most vital factors. The Psalms have both these features beyond all the other components of our liturgy. Our versicles and responses are mainly fragments of psalms. Our canticles are hymns and psalms of special or derived appropriateness. Words and music went hand in hand, and a thousand years of use brought to the early Middle Ages an art of church music of unsurpassed fitness and expression. This music fixed our intervals, our most constant melodic phrases, our cadences, and our earliest sense of melodic form. It was an art purged by devotion, serene by contemplation, warmed by communal tradition. Our music would have been something quite other than it is had not these centuries of choral use stamped it with the permanent seal of their long vocation, of their careful cloisterdom, of their essential brotherhood.

Two things defeat every historian, the slowness of time and the gradualness of change. We can record events, but we cannot record what appear to be the long and uneventful spaces between them. We cannot chronicle the thousand slight elements of a slow growth. For something like a thousand years our monasteries were the most permanent and powerful institutions in Christian Europe. The various orders arose at different times, and their aims and fortunes greatly varied, but the instinct to found and support these select and cloistered communities was one of the outstanding features of a very long period of history. Within these communities all the arts were at one time or another fostered and preserved, often to an exclusive and very high degree. A vast number of our present artistic legacies are derived from them. Of these our music is certainly one, and it is impossible either to

understand or appreciate some of its main character-
istics unless we can to some degree visualize the circumstances that gave it birth.

Plain-song or plain-chant, which was an advanced
art of melody wedded to the Latin poetry or prose of
the Church's liturgy, had already reached perfection
a thousand years ago. It remains an unsurpassed type
of musical expression. Artistic values do not depend
on complicated methods or mechanism. These single
strands of melody with which the hymns and psalms of
the Church were adorned had a fitness and beauty
which places them, simple as they are by later standards,
among the highest forms of music which inspiration has
yet devised. They remain still warm and tender,
dignified and human, and they have been strong enough
to bear an immense superstructure of more complicated ideas. Why indeed, it may be asked, were all
these subsequent elaborations necessary, if a perfect art
had already been found? The answer to that question
would explain the mystery of all creative impulses.
Men never have been content with their work, and the
more gifted they are, the less will they be satisfied.
These medieval communities were like ourselves. They
solved one problem only to meet another. There is no
finality in these things.

Slowly, uncertainly, and covering many generations
of time, they began to feel their way towards the
possible combination of one melody with another,
towards what in the course of centuries became the art
of harmony. Harmony is a unique product of our
Western music. No other music in the world shows
anything approaching it in range and organization. It
has become the essential hall-mark of our musical
sensibility. Other systems of music have made experi-

ments, some have got so far as to combine various sounds to varying degrees. But as a system complete in itself, infinitely fertile, and supporting an ever-increasing structure of concerted music of all kinds, there is elsewhere nothing fairly comparable with the art of harmony as we know it. And there is no movement in artistic history more remarkable and more challenging than this urge towards elaboration and complexity of sound which busied the minds of European musicians for centuries. Roughly from A.D. 1000 to 1500 ecclesiastical music is a long series of experiments in harmony. The length of time and wealth of resource involved in this development are a fair measure both of the persistence of the impulse and of the sustained practice on which the final results were based. Practical trial and logical theory were both concerned with it, and their interactions are illuminating.

Medieval theories of music are not unlike medieval theories of astronomy. They began with a dogma, and if the facts of experience appeared to deny it, so much the worse for the facts. The circle is a perfect figure, therefore the planets must move in circles. That was the type of argument. Planets actually move in ellipses, and observation could have proved that then as now. But theory was much too powerful, and the sky had to be filled with intricate machinery in order that the obvious details of planetary movement should not destroy the theory of the perfect circle. In just the same way were musical theorists obsessed by figures. Octaves and fifths are perfect intervals, therefore harmony must reside in octaves and fifths. The fourth is an inverted fifth. Fourths were also perfect, and a harmony consisting of moving octaves, fifths, and fourths confronts us in all the early theories of the subject. In the matter of time-values the figure three had a special, even a theological, significance, and though men marched on two feet then as now, and their hearts gave alternately a stress and a relaxation, perfect time was held to be, not the physically universal rhythm of two beats, but the theoretical one of three. In the examples and discussions which have come down to us we can see this clear conflict between theory and practice. Art is not a system of thought, but an ordered method of action. Its proper field is that of trial and error. Musicians found themselves persistently inventing new sounds, hopelessly inconsistent in theory, but strangely moving in practice.

Naturally there was strong opposition, not only from the Puritans, who distrusted all elaborations, of whatever order, but also from those who pressed a theory, or felt acutely sensitive to the simpler values. Nothing we can say of our wildest contemporaries can exceed the condemnation visited on some of these medieval pioneers of harmony. 'This music defiles the service,' wrote John of Salisbury about 1150. Pope John XXII complains in 1322, nearly two centuries later, that 'music is depraved by descants, elaborations, flourishes'. Back to plain-song, octaves, and fifths, is the cure prescribed. Meanwhile the bold spirits are preaching discords; thirds and sixths which 'make great melody'. Right or wrong, these 'discords' came to stay, and some of them are the very essence of harmony as we know it. Children at play, like soldiers on the march, will add thirds to a tune by sheer instinct. No theory of intervals, however august, can prevail against the practice of them.

It was not all pure invention, or pure instinct. The echoes of a great building, by delay and deflexion of

sound, must have accustomed men's ears to the combination of notes of considerable discordance. This
may be one of the reasons why the device of Canon,
where the same melody is sung by several voices beginning at different times, is so frequent a practice. It is
also easier, on the path of harmonic invention, to have
a known tune to hold fast. The writing of descants,
where a more definite independence of parts is deliberately contrived, was a still more fruitful origin of new
sounds. The results were often crude and clumsy, but
from time to time there occurred a passage or a cadence
so satisfying that it soon became part of all men's
musical speech. Here too there was a known melody to
hold to, in one of the parts. The other part performed
the experiments. But given a beautiful, or even a
tolerable, combination of two parts, why not three, or
four, or five? Men's voices differ in pitch. Parts having
different ranges of notes would be welcome on every
ground. The whole extent of possible vocal sounds was
gradually explored, and varieties of pitch were clothed
in varieties of melody. Vocal polyphony learnt by slow
degrees to find an effective, congenial, yet independent
use for every type of voice, and the product was extraordinarily stimulating.

It offered an inexhaustible source of expression and
adornment, and this was probably of all things the one
which its promoters most eagerly craved. The achievement of harmony is unique in our story because the
circumstances that evolved it were unique. Length and
multiplicity of devotions was a fundamental rule of the
great monastic orders. The daily round might include
Matins at midnight, when the day began, Lauds at
sunrise, Prime, Terce, Sext, and None at three-hour
intervals, Vespers at sunset, and Compline to end the

day. To these must be added the Masses which were celebrated in some communities almost without ceasing. Saints and Holy-days had their special rites. Many hours a day were normally spent in the Choir. The main outlines of the Liturgy were irrevocably fixed. Every office was sung or said times without number. Some rules included the whole of the Psalms each week. The Canticles and many of the Psalms were used every day. The language of the Church was Latin, every syllable of it familiar, yet gradually ceasing to be a living language even among those most constantly called upon to use it. And this rule of life was the foundation of thousands of communities, great and small, rich and poor, of men and of women, for hundreds of years, and in every Christian land. Is it surprising that music, once it was admitted as a possible form of enhanced expression and embellishment, became one of the main outlets for that inherently creative impulse which no severity of negation or discipline can ever permanently quell?

These monks took vows of poverty, and every founder urged this renunciation with the utmost sincerity. But nothing could prevent the gifts of faithful or grateful worshippers. The monasteries were at first rude cells, such as the hermits of older times had chosen to inhabit. They found themselves unavoidably the possessors of steadily increasing resources. They became great capitalist societies, great patrons of the arts. The cells grew into vast piles of magnificent architecture, the garden plot into a great domain. In exact parallel a simple order of worship became an elaborately expressive ritual, and in this ritual was developed the most characteristic attribute of European music, the art of harmony. The simple responses which float down to us from the choir of our cathedral are

relics of this music as the Middle Ages practised it.
The steps in its evolution, Organum in perfect intervals,
Canon employing one melody for more than one voice,
Descant finding real melodic freedom in parts, can be
studied in books and examples. So can the works of the
greater pioneers, Dunstable, Dufay, Josquin des Prés,
and their many fellow workers. The final result was
a variety in unity, a many-voiced concordance, on
which the whole marvellous wealth of sixteenth-century
vocal music was built. These pioneers are in the main
forgotten, but Palestrina knew them, and Lassus, and
Tallis and Byrd and Gibbons. The whole order of
society in which they lived and worked has gone, but
the foundations of music had been well and truly laid.

3

All music is modern when it is written. Even a composer who is following no more than a traditional path
finds something which, to him at least, is a new version
of an old truth. Contemporary taste always feels that
there is a peculiar fitness and satisfaction in the arts
which it fosters, whatever the future may think of them.
We have learnt to distinguish two main products of
medieval church music which seem to us to represent
perfection of expression within their respective spheres.
Plain-song is a mature and finished art within its chosen
limits. So is the polyphony of the sixteenth century.
But had we lived anywhere in the intervening period of
some five centuries, we should no doubt have felt every
step in the development to be a culminating point in
musical history. The first crude descants were, to those
who devised and sang them, a last revelation of beauty,
than which nothing finer could be imagined. Every age
writes up to the limits of its vision, and the appeal of its

music is deeply present and actual. It is we who find
a simple plain-chant more satisfying than a clumsy
experiment in harmony. The men who made the
experiments had no doubt of their clear superiority over
the methods of the past.

When, therefore, we extol the golden age of polyphonic vocal music, we have to remember that other
ideals were already present and active, and those who
embraced them were profoundly convinced of their
fertility and beauty. Nor is the broad line of cleavage,
between what we may call the music of the monastic
church and those other forms of religious music which
came later, merely an aesthetic divergence. It is a stark
contrast between two distinct orders of society, between
two ages which differed fundamentally in organization
and vision. The atmosphere of serene contemplation
which to our ears marks so much of the best music of the
old liturgical composers was a natural counterpart of the
cloistered way of life. Centuries of political turbulence
and material peril drove men to seek peace in another
world. Many of the rarer spirits saw no other path than
that of saving the world by renouncing it. Prayer,
poverty, and service, all voluntarily practised to the
limits of endurance, must, they felt, bring out the best
in themselves and in their surroundings alike. That was
the monastic ideal in origin, dim though it so often
became by growth of material power and privilege.
Monastic music reflected monastic ideals.

Yet there were always men of equal fervour whose
blood was too hot for contemplative inaction and discipline. Sometimes the Church absorbed them. They
became fighting saints, against evil, disease, and
tyranny. This was most frequent when communities
were young. As the monastic orders gradually acquired

wealth and material influence they became themselves part of the accepted order of things, and they tolerated abuses and injustices which their founders would have fought to the last breath. The bolder minds were driven towards reform, and the natural inertia of a great institution often drove reform into revolt. Many a loyal son of the Church, guilty only of a burning desire to fulfil her original and express commands, found himself denounced as a heretic. The vast social upheaval which on its religious side is known as the Reformation, and on its cultural side as the Renaissance, was in essence a revolt of the layman against the inert and entrenched conservatism, spiritual, intellectual, or political, of a privileged hierarchy. The ferment was rising during just those centuries when the material resources of the Church were most lavishly displayed. At the time when her arts and her music were reaching heights never before approached, a new social and political philosophy was debating the whole foundation of her order. The ornate motets of Josquin were challenged by the congregational hymns of Luther.

Of the many influences which had a share in this general ferment two are especially noteworthy, both on intellectual and artistic grounds. One was the slow decay of Latin, the other the invention of printing. Dante is to us one of the great poets. We do not think of him as a scientist, or even as a theologian. But in his own day he was in fact using all the scientific and philosophical knowledge of his time as a background for his poetic genius. His opinions, and those of the Italian writers and poets who succeeded him, were opinions on what were then held to be matters of historical and scientific fact. These discussions were written in Italian, and Italian at once became a language of the first order.

Great problems which had hitherto been examined almost exclusively in scholastic Latin were brought out into the daylight of a living speech. They became topics of wide and informed discussion among all classes of educated men, and among many more whose education was thus first stimulated. Religion and politics, art, music, and drama, all found themselves subject to vivid analysis and debate. Even in the field of classical literature itself, there appeared a formidable rival to Latin. Greek was rediscovered and brought with it the seething ideas and problems of the ancient Greek poets and philosophers. Greek scholars were brought to Italy and a fierce controversy arose in the universities of Europe as to whether Greek might or might not be admitted as a field of study comparable in a measure with the overwhelming claims of the Latinists. It is curious to reflect to-day that Greek was held, so comparatively recently, to be an unwarranted intruder in the academic groves.

In England Chaucer and Wycliffe were contemporaries, the one writing a panorama of English life and character which gave power and relish both to social thought and to vivid native speech, the other translating and interpreting the Bible in order that men might study it at first hand. In view of its enormous quantity, medieval art was very restricted in subject-matter. Lively and beautiful as it so often was, it yet touched only a small fraction of the sacred texts, and a very large number of what to us are the most important Biblical incidents and ideas were apparently quite unknown to the artists of the Middle Ages. The discovery and dissemination of the whole Bible was by far the most signal influence which moulded the intellectual character of the religious reformers. And this influence was inseparably connected with the use of living languages.

Men might misunderstand the message. They could no longer ignore it.

Printing had already come when Luther's countrymen discovered the power of their own language and of the whole Bible almost simultaneously. Thereafter nothing could stop the march of knowledge and the communication of ideas, and in this fever of discussion and discovery the whole society of literate men and women could claim a share. In every sphere the spirit of exploration was triumphant. Columbus challenged the seas while Copernicus measured the heavens. Erasmus searched the minds and motives, while Luther purged the souls of men.

Nor were these searchings without marked effect on those who clung most tenaciously to the old order. The schisms and scandals of the Roman Church had been too notorious for her sincerest friends to gloss over. She had permitted the death of a Savonarola, and prosecuted with medieval fury a policy of repression, but she took steps to put her own house in some degree of order. Councils and decrees were frequent and drastic, and the most famous of these active inquiries, the Council of Trent, had artistic as well as ecclesiastical ideals. The music of the Church had often tended towards an ornate and incongruous extravagance not unlike that which disfigured the lives of some of her prelates. The Council of Trent noted these things and resolved to adopt simpler and purer fashions of art. The music of Palestrina is an echo of these thoughts. It is by common consent the summit of sacred musicianship of the Roman allegiance. It is the last and finest fruit of five centuries of effort, purged of extravagance, perfect in taste and craftsmanship, sustained in nobility and serene emotion. It remains a model of all that was best in the cloistered church, but it was the last of its kind to win a universal tribute. Thereafter the development of the best church music passes in the main beyond the Alps. The future lay with Germany and its reformed Church.

Our own great Tudor school derived much of its character from Italy, but it had distinctive features of its own. There is in general a more bracing atmosphere, well suited to our climate and our speech. Our composers as a whole cared less for the impeccable smoothness of technique found in the best Italians. They are bolder and more angular, and not rarely deliberately harsh in the pursuit of original harmonies and in the illustration of verbal ideas. They were much nearer to the reformed text, and had their inspiration persisted they might well have achieved a synthesis between the past and the future. Their best works have a truth and directness of expression second to nothing in the whole range of music. But they were living on the edge of social and religious revolutions. They survived Palestrina by one generation and then their art perished in the conflicts of the sects.

4

German sacred music is founded on the Chorale, a broad congregational melody allied to a versified psalm or hymn. It is the insurgence of the nave in religious worship, and this in two ways. The nave will itself take part, but it will also listen intently for whatever message of inspiration or emphasis may be given by music to the literal text. The whole congregation sings its hymns, and the more specialized musicians, choir and organist, are expected to produce a music of their own, designed not solely for those who take an active part in it, but calculated also to make clear to the listeners the devotional or dramatic character of the chosen words. Protestant anthem and cantata are sung by the choir, but they are addressed to the nave. They must use a living language, and must try to interpret it adequately.

If a thousand people are to sing together, some form of musical discipline is essential. Melodies must move slowly and broadly, and there must be a frame of rhythm that will give the tune an appreciable pulse and form. In the matter of words too, the freedom of prose will not do. That is why the Psalms were put into metrical versions. The singing of Psalms in prose defeated, and still defeats, large congregations. The Anglican Church tries, by a free reciting-note followed by a bar or two of more formal melody, to make the best of both worlds, but only the highly trained can sing prose unanimously, and normal congregations must be content either to listen to the choir or follow it very tentatively. The Scots Psalter is a more consistent solution. The Psalms are ingeniously versified, and fitted to dignified congregational tunes. There are no difficulties of pace or metre, and the result is devotional music which every one can sing. The German Chorale uses exactly the same methods. The tunes themselves must be of suitable compass, and they must have no undue angularity either of pitch or rhythm. Above all, they must not attempt too much emotional or dramatic detail. The words are regular in metre and accent, but the verses vary in meaning. The tune has to fit them all impartially, and it should therefore express a general rather than a particular mood. Most of the unsatisfactory hymn-tunes are the fruit of a short-sighted desire to be moving or literal in the expression of detail. The tunes which have survived to be universally accepted in Protestant Europe are without exception dignified in style, smooth in melody, and steady in rhythm. They suit all kinds of voices, and every corporate mood of worship. They give us, perhaps for the first time in history, a truly democratic art.

The laymen not only brought their voices to the Church, they brought their instruments too. There is no doubt that the early Church was compelled to frown on instrumental music, if only by reason of its pagan associations. Moreover, from a purely musical point of view, most instruments were for long very crude in structure and could not begin to compete with the voice, either in quality of tone or range of expression. They were thus both secular in atmosphere and inferior in musical aptitude. Serious music, up to the time of the Reformation, is almost exclusively vocal. Reform brought all kinds of new influences, some transitory or incongruous, some permanent. In village and town where local musicians were to be found, their instruments began to appear and take a part in church music on festal or special occasions. This practice has survived almost to our own day, and there have been many conservative and isolated communities which contrived to withstand, for many generations, the almost universal adoption of the organ as the specifically religious instrument.

The organ can be traced back to quite early in the Middle Ages. We read of cumbrous mechanisms with many bellows, great levers for keys, and stentorian pipes. They seem to have been more astonishing than musical. In any case there was as yet no place for the organ as we know it. There was no music for it. So long as music was mainly one line of melody, it could never occur even to the most fertile inventor to do more

than these early organs did; namely, reinforce one note
at a time. Harmony had to come, before the possibility
of a handy keyboard, suited to the playing of chords and
simultaneous parts, could be thought of. With the
development of harmony the keyboard rapidly assumed
great importance, and the organ then began to find its
way into every religious community which had the skill
and wealth to construct one. The organist could there
play all the parts in a complicated texture. The sustained tone of the instrument, together with its size and
fitness for large spaces, made it the ideal medium for
ceremonial effect. Its very lack of detailed expression
made it admirably fitted to carry on the traditions of
serenity and dignity so long associated with religious
music. It soon became itself so rich in sacred memory
and allusion that it was one of the most potent aids to
the music of worship. That atmosphere it has permanently retained.

The first great organ school arose in Italy. Vocal
harmonies were the framework of its music, but the
Italians progressed with fine originality into the realm
of a new and more instrumental style. They could take
a plain-song as theme, and by means of the larger
compass, the contrasted tones, and the flexibility of
finger natural to the keyboard, could develop and em-
bellish it far beyond the range of voices. This art they
taught to their German pupils, who found in the reformed Church at home a wonderful field for the exercise of these powers. Nothing could be better suited to
this artistic treatment than the Chorale-tunes which
every one knew and loved. Nowhere is the essential
grandeur, permanence, and fruitfulness of broadly
conceived melody more manifest. There are thousands
of these Chorale Preludes for the organ, of every type

and mood. Some are worthy to rank with the greatest instrumental forms. Some, like the so-called 'Giant' Fugue of Bach, have reached world-wide familiarity. All are proof of the unique and abiding place which the Lutheran hymn had taken in Protestant music. From this time on, the sacred music of Germany is suffused with the warmth and nobility of these tunes. Their inflexions and cadences become the alphabet of her church musicians.

The music written for Protestant choirs used the various native translations of Bible, prayer-book, and hymns. The developing musical fashions of Opera and Oratorio, which we shall have to discuss later, were not slow to point the way to a musical treatment of the literal prose of the Bible. Simple settings of prose to a flexible succession of notes for a single voice might enhance the meaning of the words without altogether losing either the accents or the clarity of speech. In Passion music and Cantata it was possible to keep very close to the natural flow of prose by using this type of musical narration. Recitative, as it is called, is not difficult to follow if the words are already fairly familiar to the listener. The practice was in essence the same use of inflexion and cadence which had been imposed on liturgical Latin many centuries before. This musical Latin had remained fairly simple and intelligible so long as the Latin itself had kept its conventional pace and pronunciation, and it had in early times been tolerably well understood by those who sang it. But a living language is a far more powerful means of expression than a dead one, however venerable. Words in daily use cannot so easily be made into vocal exercises. They must always tend to retain a reasonable share of their natural shapes and values, and this is a healthy check on thoughtless emphasis and ornamentation. If in addition the words are taken from a text accounted literally sacred, the recited form should normally observe the rules of a simple artistic dignity. It was this plain telling of a story in music which held together the various elements in sacred music of narrative or descriptive type.

Two distinct uses of the chorus were also possible. It could personify the Apostles, or the soldiers, or the crowd of Jews, interjecting those words which were recorded as having been used by a number of people. This was an obvious dramatic effect of great power. And the chorus could also be used to represent the whole body of Christian worshippers. It could sing a devotional or contemplative number which expressed the feelings of the general congregation of believers at any suitable moment in the unfolding of the story. This practice was in very close touch with the past, and it helped to transfer to the Protestant churches some of that atmosphere of reflective devotion which was characteristic of the best monastic music. It was that same art of the choir, select in skill and sympathy, yet turned more definitely, by the use of a living language, towards the expectant and understanding ear of the whole body of the Church.

All these features of a new and more congregational form of worship found their most fruitful soil in Germany, where an intense fervour of reform was allied to native seriousness of character and to a musical sensitiveness of remarkable depth and extent. Many generations of her organists, now mostly forgotten, devoted themselves to providing music of this reformed and congregational yet eminently sacred character. They played their Chorales, they accompanied the congregation, and they used their more trained singers and players to provide musical settings of Psalms and sacred stories, devised so as to throw into relief the chief incidents, but never losing touch with the essentially corporate aim of the whole method. For it must never be forgotten that the German Passions and Cantatas were in the strictest sense religious services. They were not sacred concerts. Hymns and Psalms, prayers and sermons, musical narrative and reflection, were all parts of a general and congregational order of worship, in which every person present had an active and appropriate share to fulfil. This brought the congregation, the organ, the choir, and such orchestral instruments as were at hand, into an intimate and religious community of purpose such as had never before been achieved. We are beginning to appreciate the unique and lasting character of this music by our growing attention to the Passions and Cantatas of Bach. At a distance of two hundred years his work stands out above all his predecessors and contemporaries, but he was one only of a very large number of men working to these ideals. The summit of their beauty is found in Bach, but he was, no less than Palestrina, the culminating point of a long tradition. He was the glorious end of two centuries of effort.

Bach learnt his organ-playing from men whose predecessors had inherited what was best in the pioneer school of Italy. He applied it as they did to his beloved Chorales and to great detached pieces of analogous style. He provided for his choir and orchestra music of the prevailing religious type. There is in him a supreme combination of all that a thousand years of church music had developed, but he invented hardly at all. He found a method of sacred composition and used it consummately. The details of his protestant environment were already fixed. These he applied, in reflective choruses, in sacred narrative, in dramatic contrast, and in the adornment of congregational hymns. We perform his Cantatas to-day, sometimes in a church, sometimes in a concert-hall. In both places they are, to us, sacred concerts. They were not concerts to Bach. They were to him what High Mass was to Palestrina. Instead of the priestly offices of the Mass, the Lutheran cantata had its preacher and his sermon. Instead of the catholic congregation passively receptive of a priestly blessing, there was an active body of worshippers, listening to suitable homilies and singing its own praises in its own tongue. The Mass is in perpetual danger, now as in the Middle Ages, of becoming by elaboration more and more remote from the universal expression of a general devotion. That could not so easily happen to Bach's services, because the congregation was an integral and controlling part of them. Organ, orchestra, choir, and soloists might display a specialized art, but at every pause in the narrative the whole congregation with corporate voice gave the occasion its living and present acceptance. Its hymns were the background against which the more highly organized music was projected. The thoughts thus expressed in its own language determined the character of the whole service, both as a profession of faith and as the practice of an art. Bach's music comes neither from the cloister nor from the study. It is a layman's worship, written with the fervour of an evangel, and with the skill of genius.

5

Those branches of the Church which remained true to the Roman allegiance did not escape the democratic infection, but their response to it took a different and

less consistent form. The laity were not actively in-
corporated in the services, after the German fashion,
but a very definite appeal was made to their artistic
sense. Sacerdotal tradition was too strong to permit an
integral co-operation of all the members of the Church
in its use and government, but the Church began to
import from outside the musical resources which were
so rapidly accumulating in other spheres. Palestrina
was the end of the old era. After his death all the more
active spirits turned to the theatre, and the rising tide of
Opera was by far the most potent musical influence in
seventeenth-century Italy. When the Church wished
to add to its own more traditional resources, the appeal
of the new dramatic music was irresistible. This new
music had its own problems, but for the moment we are
concerned with their reactions in the Church. The
temptation to use the new dramatic technique in all
music, whether sacred or secular, could not be with-
stood, and when the Church set out to enlarge its
musical horizon, it found itself borrowing wholesale
from the theatre. Composers, players, and singers were
brought over from their daily occupation with the stage,
and encouraged to give the Church a taste of those new
methods of musical expression which practice in the
theatre had taught them.

It is clear that many of the most sensitive composers were uncomfortable under this system. They frequently show a most curious diversity of styles. They
seem to have felt that the operatic method was not really
convincing in the old sacred surroundings. Writing, as
they often did, for voices only, they retained much of
the purity and serenity of atmosphere which belonged
to the old order. When, however, they were com-
missioned to employ the whole musical apparatus of

the theatre, soloists, chorus, and orchestra, they found it impossible to resist those technical devices which the stage had suggested. The same composer would write church music in one style for one occasion, and church music of a totally different type for another. And there was unfortunately no doubt which the congregation liked best. Prelates and people both demanded just those kinds of musical effect which they heard and applauded in the theatre. The result was that the older church music, so truly consonant with the deepest religious aspirations, began to appear outworn, while its place was taken by what in secular surroundings was a form of dramatic entertainment. And a dramatic entertainment it remained, whether within the Church or outside it.

To St. Jerome, in ancient days, is attributed the saying that 'a Christian maiden ought not even to know what a flute is'. This sentiment must be interpreted in the light of those Pagan festivals of instrumental music which were often accompanied by less admirable features which the early Church so passionately opposed. Zealous saints were acutely conscious that a custom perfectly innocent in itself may by evil association bring very undesirable practices in its train. That was why St. Jerome, in common with many later saints, drew what appears to be so arbitrary a line between flutes and voices. Could he have watched the fashions of Italian church music in the seventeenth and eighteenth centuries, he would have felt the wisdom of his attitude to be only too abundantly proved. Apart from the growing use of the organ, there was no such thing as sacred instrumental music. The Italian orchestra was formed and trained in the theatre, and it could not suddenly become something else when it walked over

to the Church. The famous solo singers equally belonged to the stage. There they had learnt the arts
of public performance. They could not change their
methods by stepping from a secular to a sacred platform.
Composers might be given sacred words to set, but
these words were Latin, often but dimly or crudely
understood, and the natural attitude to words of every
kind became that which was daily adopted in the
theatre. To composers, as to their patrons, there was
every temptation to use that type of music which was
so warmly acclaimed by the public support of opera.
Given the means of the theatre, they adopted the
theatrical style, and the record of their work is a record
of the progressive degeneration of elaborate sacred
offices until they became little more than a fashionable
entertainment. Appeal to a thoughtless public taste had
met with its invariable fate. It reached the lowest
common standard of value.

The contrast between the church music of Italy and
that of Germany, during the hundred and fifty years
which separated Bach from Palestrina, is extraordinarily
vivid. There is not, on the surface, such a very great
difference of means. The Germans developed a strong
feeling for dramatic representation of ideas in music,
and they employed soloists, chorus, and orchestra. But
these things grew up within the Church itself, and that
Church had both the strength of its reforming piety and
the impregnable rock of its translated Bible. It was also
a democratic Church, not only in public appeal, but in
actual foundation. The Church in Italy was popular
enough. People flocked to hear its elaborate concerts.
But the German congregation was very much more than
an audience. It had passed through fire and sword to
reach a conscious ideal of religious faith and freedom.

That ideal touched the humblest as well as the greatest of its sons. The music of Bach was its artistic embodiment. Elsewhere the quality of church music was clearly in decline long before Bach was born. It is a still further tribute to him and to his countrymen that they pursued their own high aims with such continued integrity.

The decline was not confined to Italy. Our English diarist Evelyn could write in 1663:

'One of His Majesty's chaplains preached; after which, instead of the ancient, grave, and solemn wind music accompanying the organ, was introduced a concert of twenty-four violins between every pause, after the French fantastical light way, better suiting to a tavern, or playhouse, than a church.'

France, Austria, and Catholic Germany caught the contagion, and during the course of the eighteenth century the fashionable Masses written and used in the most august surroundings were often of a shallowness and incongruity beyond belief. The dance-tunes, the orchestral ritornelli, the vocal flourishes, the pseudo-dramatic choruses, all were frankly transported from the theatre to the church, and every serious contemporary witness has testified to a growing degradation of taste. So popular was the importation, so influentially supported, that Europe has hardly yet recovered from it, and of its baneful consequences there is at least one overwhelming proof. Since the operatic movement arose in Italy in the seventeenth century, no liturgical work of supreme quality has been written within that Church. Bach's Mass in B minor was not written for liturgical use, nor has it been so used. Beethoven's Mass in D is a sacred symphony, also written outside the Church. Mozart's Requiem Mass has the poignancy of his last days, but what is the repute of all the conventional Masses which he and the two Haydns and Schubert wrote? They are less convincing works of their respective composers. Genius itself could do nothing with the style of church music prevailing in their day.

Reformers, and there have been many, have long been thoroughly alive to these facts. Facile melody, conventional choruses and glib orchestration do not make church music, even at the hands of great talent. Reform in every country finds itself returning to the sixteenth century, to the schools of Palestrina and the Tudors, when what is felt to be the truest idiom of the old Catholic worship last found expression.

Nor are the Protestant churches in much better case. Since Bach died in 1750, no great master has found work for his whole talent within the Protestant communion. A few truly devotional works, like the German Requiem of Brahms, were written outside it. So were all the great sacred epics of the concert-room. The Church borrows from these masterpieces. She no longer creates them. And there are only two possible explanations of this artistic dearth. Either no musician of supreme endowment has found himself in the service of the Church, a chance so improbable that it may be dismissed, or else the Church has consistently failed to offer a sensitive ear and an adequate scope for his genius. Bach's gifts died with him. Not for a century after his death did they win external tribute. Like Palestrina, he had no true successors, and the new fashions of musical display buried his work for generations. One clear example of this blindness to real artistic and devotional values may be seen in quite recent times, and very near home.

When, towards the end of the nineteenth century, an influential section of the Anglican Church began to advocate and develop a more ornate liturgical ceremonial, it was not to Palestrina, or Byrd, or Bach, that they turned for appropriate music. They imported Masses of the later Italian order, sometimes further sentimentalized by passage through France, and they offered these showy productions as the principal musical ornaments of an English Choral Communion. We need not wonder at the naiveties of a village church cantata. Such crude and theatrical ideas were not invented in the remote countryside. Their models were sung and endorsed by fashionable metropolitan churches, by people who claimed to be in the van of ecclesiastical and artistic progress. They did not lack sincerity. What they lacked was knowledge. Religious music, like religious ritual, should come spontaneously from within, and it should express, not a temporary or superficial appeal to the ear, but a devotion of the whole mind, as deep and as disciplined as the ancient liturgy itself.

6

Such, in broadest outline, has been the place of music as handmaid to the Church. Our English cathedral can teach us much about these varied ideals of the past, for her unbroken historical continuity has kept traces of them all. That continuity has also saved her from being the exclusive servant of any temporary fashion, however powerful. Her versicles and responses, her chanted canticles and psalms, are echoes of the Middle Ages. Her congregational hymns are products of the Reformation and of some subsequent revivals. There are hymns translated from early or medieval

Latin. There are hymns from the rediscovered Greek. A large number come from Germany and from the Scots Psalter. Many have been culled from the poets, or written to express ethical ideals. Her tunes are equally varied. A few belong in spirit to the plain-song of the Middle Ages. Many more, and these of the best, are German Chorales or Scots psalm-tunes. There is also a fine group of specifically English tunes, mostly from the eighteenth century, which are as dignified as the German, yet show the definitely native love of a strong rolling rhythm. The Methodist revival of the early nineteenth century stimulated a much needed revival in the Anglican Church itself. The hymns of the Wesleys came into the Church, and so, unfortunately, did many later revivalist tunes. Missionary fervour was held to excuse excess of sentiment and crude musicianship. Some of the popular hymn-tunes of the nineteenth century were the musical equivalent of a too fervid oratory. They illustrate the historical fact that all the worst religious music has been written by two classes of writer. The one is without any genuinely religious emotion whatever. The other has nothing else. The abysmal Masses of the eighteenth century were written by musicians of poor religious taste. Much of the music of our nineteenth century was written by evangelists sadly deficient in musical taste.

The Anglican anthem is our equivalent for the Latin motet of Rome on the one hand, and the German cantata on the other. The Latin motets were of the polyphonic school, using the perfect vocal technique of the liturgy to adorn select passages of the Latin Bible and prayer-book. Our great Tudor anthems apply this same method to the English text. It survives in Tallis, Byrd, Gibbons, and their contemporaries, whose

music now claims a growing favour; and it is frequently
imitated, with a wider harmonic horizon, by modern
writers. We have never adopted the German cantata as
a whole, but the narrative and descriptive features of it
are found in a large proportion of our anthems. Purcell
is the first great representative of the post-Reformation
style which for so long supplanted the old liturgical music
almost completely. He, like the Italians, worked largely
in the theatre, but his taste was saved from the most
serious lapses by two causes. His genius was too original
and too fertile to follow a commonplace convention
rigidly, and he was held, both by education and by the
conditions of his work, very close to the sacred text.
No composer ever had a finer sense of the value of
words. His words were of the English Bible, and not
even a Restoration court could ignore their inspired
grandeur. To the people as a whole they were of clear
and divine portent, and Purcell at his best was worthy
of them. His free use of soloists is in tune with the new
fashions of his time. So are his frequent orchestral
interludes. We rarely hear his church music as he
wrote it, but it has many permanent beauties.

Thereafter English church music fell into a back-
water, and who shall say, in view of what happened
elsewhere, that this was not a partial blessing? We
lacked the German intensity, but we were spared the
Italian shallowness. Many generations of competent
organists continued to write services and anthems of
undistinguished, but at the same time of solid and
useful, quality. A few, like the Wesleys, had flashes of
real genius. Sebastian Wesley is probably a clear case
of a man who, had he enjoyed the opportunities given
to some of the great men abroad, would have made
masterpieces of European repute. His gifts would

have filled a much broader sphere, had the English Church of his time possessed the means fitly to employ him. The less talented men, though rarely inspired, never lost a fair sense of religious fitness, and to them also the majestic English of the services was a constant education and safeguard. Moreover, in spite of revolution and dissent, both within and without, the English Church retained, and still retains, much of the internal organization of the Middle Ages. Canons, clergy, and choir still sit in the same order, and often in the same carved stalls, which their monastic predecessors occupied. Our choir still consists of lay clerks and boys.

It often surprises our Protestant kinsmen abroad that we have clung so tenaciously to this narrow view of the type of voice appropriate to the Church. Our men altos in particular seem to some of our visitors strange and unnatural. But the Anglican choir is a monastic survival, and with it have survived these traditions of monastic music. The passionless tone of boys' voices suits the passionless serenity of contemplative worship. Our altos are trained to produce the nearest equivalent to that smooth and restful tone. Mellowed by the echoes of a great building, it is in spirit the oldest music we know. The Anglican choir is not a choral society. It is a special and delicate instrument for the production of special and delicate effects, and it has fifteen hundred years of proved experience behind it. We have seen what happened to those churches which imported the prima-donna and the operatic chorus instead. We have no reason to envy them. Our cathedral organist, with his men and boys, may have made no great mark in the world, but he and they have preserved an atmosphere, bequeathed from the long past, which carries with it an ideal of religious and musical intimacy not easily to be matched in our less restful age. The Anglican anthem, written for this special choir, may be but a modest contribution to the story of music, but it is often a very fragrant one.

As for the organ itself, we owe to it more than we are wont to realize. For the mass of men, and for many generations, it was the most serious instrumental music they could know. It was the training-ground of innumerable musicians, both here and abroad, and the significance of its influence is shown by the fact that so many of our chief institutional appointments have for centuries been the accepted preserve of the organist. Cathedrals, universities, and schools have all made the organ-loft the centre of their musical life, and many of them, but for the organ, might never have admitted music at all, on anything approaching its present integral status. This custom too is monastic in origin and goes very deeply into our sense of fitness. When a new college or school builds a chapel and installs an organ, it is obeying an instinct which has its roots in the monastic schools of the Middle Ages, and this tradition is stronger in England than anywhere else because the initial concentration of religion, education, and art under the same endowments has never been completely broken. Classical organ-music owes much of its character to this long association. Ordered worship and educated taste have spared it much meretricious handling. 'Orchestral' organ-playing is a modern notion, more ingenious than convincing. Mechanism can now offer a play-box of queer stops and restless combinations which are often thoroughly retrograde. They may serve an ephemeral purpose in other places, but they do not belong to the art of classical organ-playing, as generations of fine organists have taught it. The organ was evolved for broad effects. It also demands impeccable clarity of taste. Then, and only then, is it in tune with its noblest traditions.

The history of English church music is not an inglorious one. It had a fair share in the Tudor masterpieces, and that was only the summit of what had been a very long period of discovery and achievement. If, since then, it has created little, it has preserved much. It still gives us what, as part of the whole church of Western Christendom in the Middle Ages, it helped to create, a glimpse of the abiding foundations of our music. As we pursue the further story of the art we shall have to admit that most of the later masterpieces have been evolved elsewhere, and the question arises as to whether the essentially creative spirit of music will ever return again to its earlier haunts; to those great cathedrals, for example, near one of which we have spent this discursive hour? Must Cantata and Oratorio be consigned, more often than not, to the concert-hall, while the great churches and cathedrals pursue their more exclusive path? A few have opened their doors, but these wonderful buildings, which by magnificence and tradition should house all the masterpieces of every art, are too often empty and silent. Some of her own music the Church retains. Her walls are periodically filled by the corporate devotions of her own people. But will she ever again become the mother of all endeavour, the home of all sorts and conditions of artists, of all professions and denominations, bringing the best they can do? Will the great orchestral symphonies ever find a natural home in the wide spaces of her nave? Will the ethereal beauty of a string quartet secure a corner in one of her transepts? These are questions to which the Church herself can alone find answer.

CASTLE AND CHAMBER

CASTLE AND CHAMBER

I

THE arts of ancient Greece, no less than the conquests of ancient Rome, belonged to a social order which held slavery to be a normal feature of civilization. There had to be hewers of wood and drawers of water, and it seemed a natural economy to reserve a special and permanent supply of labour for these essential services. Artists and philosophers, soldiers, merchants, lawyers, and administrators, all alike needed material means for the pursuit of their aims, and it appeared only common sense to give absolute command of labour to those whose business it was to direct it in the service of society. Neither the saints nor the philosophers ever seriously challenged the custom, nor did the slaves themselves rebel, so long as they were given the maintenance and protection which their enforced status deserved. The gist of many an ancient precept is not so much that slavery is inherently wrong in system, as that ownership must accept responsibility, and that masters should have a care for their slaves not differing too widely from a parent's care for his children. This, no doubt, was an ideal only rarely reached in practice, but the many cases of slaves who were carefully trained, and given positions of high power and trust, show that there were at least a fair number of masters who interpreted their duties generously. It was the selfish and irresponsible owner who brought discredit on the system and prepared men for its overthrow. It was the rulers who degenerated rather than the ruled.

The same social convenience, the same conditional stability, and the same ultimate degeneration marks the serfdom of the Middle Ages. A few of us may, in simple faith, cherish our Norman blood, but the vast majority of our ancestors were serfs, living under conditions and restrictions not far removed from slavery. There was, however, a vital difference between serfdom and slavery, which in theory at least was plain and acknowledged. The slave had no legal claims on his master, but the feudal system, from the King at its head to the serf at its foundation, was a professed chain of mutual duties and services. The vassal owed service and loyalty to his lord, but the lord equally owed protection and maintenance to his vassals. At its best there was a kinship and devotion between all the members of a feudal order which made it a powerful instrument of government. It also, in turbulent times, offered a fair prospect of stability and prosperity. Even the serf could see that this ordered tyranny was preferable to the banditry of war and anarchy. Though he often paid a heavy price for a doubtful security, the serf learnt to feel and recognize certain loyalties which had stood the strain of lesser feuds and factions, and he expressed these thoughts through many an old song and story.

Slaves have always been singers. The monotony of toil will make the most primitive beings break into a croon or chant. If the labour is rhythmic, then the rhythm will give impulse and form to the song. We owe the character of many of our loveliest melodies to the monotonous rocking of a cradle, and there is a whole literature of fine songs which grew out of the rhythmic hauling of a rope. The sea shanty is only a later and more specialized example of the chants of those ancient toilers who rowed the galleys of the Mediterranean. Even if labour is not in itself rhythmic, monotony will tend to make it so in feeling. The worker will relieve his own tension by some form of rhythmic action which will serve at least to help the march of time. From this it is but a step to express thoughts that may wander over the whole field of fate and circumstance. This is why so many old folk-melodies, though they may speak of recreation rather than labour, yet have an under-current of melancholy. Centuries of exhausting and monotonous work will give a tinge of sadness to arts which in themselves were an escape from that bondage, a faint but unquenchable hope for better things.

A vivid illustration of these reactions is to be found in the music of the negro slaves of America. This music expresses their hopes and fears, their toils and pleasures, in an idiom at first borrowed from their masters. These negro melodies are not African in origin. They are European music modified by contact with the African mind. These slaves, thus expressing the pathos of their fate and the crude imagery of their hopes, have produced a form of art which has had notable influence on the taste of their masters. They have infected many social circles as far removed from slavery as could well be imagined. The incongruity of Negro Spirituals in a European drawing-room does not alter the fact that they are the sincerest possible expressions of a hard life and a primitive creed. Denied the fruits of this world, the slave all the more eagerly welcomed those features of his master's religion which appeared to promise compensation, both material and spiritual, in the next. His status gave these images their poignancy, his primitive mind gave them their crudity. His native heritage of dancing, the most fundamental of all ritual instincts, clothed his melodies in strong rhythms, or led him to choose those European tunes which could most easily be modified in this direction.

This negro music is in essence very close to some of the earliest and most primitive forms of folk-music that we know. Its ingenuous literalism of thought is very near to that of the European slaves and serfs of our own past. The untutored mind can only grasp an event or a truth in terms which are within its own understanding. It is a common experience of teachers and missionaries that the child will return a childish answer, the savage a crude image, however exalted the truth which is being taught them. Stories and precepts, if they are to be grasped at all, must be brought within the simpler ambit of the pupil's own mind. The results are often disconcerting, but as often disarming, in their unreserved and literal confidence. It was a medieval shepherd who sang to the Babe in the manger:

> Hail! Sweet is thy cheer;
> My heart woulde bleed
> To see thee sit here
> In so poore weed,
>   With no pennies.

> Hail! Put forth thy dall!
> I bring thee but a ball!
> Have and play thee withal,
>   And go to the tennis!

The daily battle of the European serf was with nature rather than with men. The demands on his labour were incessant and exacting, but if only nature would smile, increasing the crops and multiplying the herds, then life might be tolerable. He had to live in a hovel with his own or his lord's cattle. Coarse food and rough clothing were the best he could hope for. For warmth and light he depended on the sun and seasons. Yet with all these privations, the material gulf between him and his lord was not necessarily so great as it has since been between the very rich and the very poor. The lord lived in a castle, but this castle was a fortress rather than a house. Of comfort and convenience in our modern sense it had none. It was big enough to house a small army and solid enough to stand a siege. But the hall was strewn with rushes and befouled by dogs. Dirt and disease took the same heavy toll from lord and peasant alike. The 'plague, pestilence, and famine' of our Litany were not remote or empty words. Of 'battle, murder, and sudden death' the lord might well have a special share. He held great powers over his subjects, but his equals and superiors could exact extreme penalties from him.

It was in building these enormous feudal strongholds that masons learnt how to build churches and abbeys. Our domestic architecture begins with a fortress. These castles have lost their original purpose even more completely than the monasteries, but they were in their day the outward symbol of an essential need. They might overawe the country-side, but they also served to protect it.

There are thus two main strands of thought in the poetry and song most characteristic of the Middle Ages. One is the sense of absolute dependence on nature. The other is the value of personal courage and loyalty. The love-songs of troubadours belong to a comparatively restricted and artificial society. They might beguile the idle hours of a well-protected court. But what stirred the deepest chords of sympathy in all men, without distinction, were the visible and tangible gifts of nature, and the heroic stories of personal and tribal adventure. The lyric songs are of nature:

Winter wakenth all my care . . . .

E

Groweth seed, and bloweth mead,
And spring'th the woode new . . .

Pleasure it is
To hear, y-wis,
The birdes sing.
The deer in the dale,
The sheep in the vale,
The corn springing . . .

Such lines are of the essence of medieval poetry. It is not the serene contemplation of nature, but a passionate longing for her more gracious and fertile moods. The reflective poetry of nature comes very much later in social history, and it comes, to put it baldly, from a full larder rather than from an empty one. What we find grand and inspiring our ancestors found forbidding and terrible. What fills us with the joy of well-being gave them an acute hunger for nature's fruits. Behind them lay the rigours of a winter without light or warmth or palatable food. Before them lay the ever-present risk of famine. Famine in medieval Europe was like famine in modern Asia, frequent and irremediable.

When the larder was full, men turned to more ribald themes. Love, courtship, and the accidents, rather than the sanctities, of marriage. Food, particularly the spoils of the poacher, was a welcome subject, and drink, if it were strong enough. They cheated the steward in song, and chaffed the priest. They danced to a pipe or fiddle. The peasant knew nothing either of comfort or privacy. His pleasures were food and drink, the season's dance, the topical song, and a good deal of rough horse-play. The Church tried in vain to keep her holy-days sober. Life was uncertain and very hard, and in the intervals of his toil the peasant longed for a material rather than for an ecclesiastical feast.

In times of peace and plenty he might find many an open entertainment at the castle, and watch the sports of his superiors. The pleasures of the castle were often no less crude and material than his own, but there was a more ceremonious hospitality, and a chance of more skilled entertainment. The repute and emoluments of minstrelsy in feudal times throw a strong sidelight on the taste and recreations of the baronial castle. Minstrels appear to have included every type of entertainer, from the trick juggler to the epic poet. They formed a guild of great power and status. Laws were made for their recognition and protection. The most famous of them travelled with a retinue, received a stately welcome and generous rewards. They were often treated as the equals of their noblest patrons. They fulfilled many purposes which were of high importance in a complicated but unlettered society. They were chroniclers, confidants, newsagents, ambassadors. A gifted minstrel could put a story into verse, a verse into song. He could enhance a personal reputation and rouse a local or national ardour. His stories and ballads were the repositories of history and tradition. He could help a reigning house by filling men with passionate loyalty for it. He was of all men the most welcome at the greater feasts of the castle. He played and sang and jested to the delight of the whole company, and was a social instrument of very great value. He kept men in touch with other scenes and customs. He knew strange houses and distant kinsmen.

There were a great many vagrant imitators of less reputable type, and with the spread of secular learning the profession of minstrel decayed, like that of some of the wandering clerks who were ecclesiastical only in name, until it became an ignominy rather than an

honour. But in its best days it was an influential con-
fraternity of players, story-tellers, poets, and musicians,
and we have many echoes of its achievements in the
heroic ballads and tender lyrics which have come down
to us anonymously. Of the minstrel's curious mixture
of song, jest, and wisdom, the Court fool of Shakespeare
is an example. He was the butt and yet the equal of his
master. He could disguise in a jest an unpalatable truth
that the King's counsellors dare not utter, and he could
soften it with a song that might ease the cares both of
his own and of his master's lot.

> He that hath and a tiny little wit,
> With hey, ho, the wind and the rain,
> Must make content with his fortunes fit,
> For the rain it raineth every day.

Chaucer tells us something of the instruments of his
time, the fourteenth century. The Squire 'singing he
was, and fluting all the day'. The mendicant Friar 'had
a merry note; Well could he sing and playen on a rote'.
'A bag-pipe could he (The Miller) blow and sound.'
The rote was a form of lyre, the strings being plucked
like those of a harp. There were possibilities of simple
harmony, but it was not until the lute came, with its
finger-board, that a varied harmony began to be really
practicable. Primitive harps have few strings, and they
were used in the main to pick out the single notes of a
tune. The drone of the bag-pipe had a suggestion of
harmony in it, but it was and still is very crude, apart
from the pierced pipe which could play melodies. So
long as music was mainly melody, instruments were
also melodic. The 'flute, cornet, sackbut, psaltery,
dulcimer' of the Bible were not so much exact equiva-
lents for the obscure words used in the Hebrew story of

Nebuchadnezzar, but free translations that would be understood by men of the reformed church in England. The cornet was a wind instrument with keys; the sackbut was the precursor of the trombone; the psaltery was a simple harp; the dulcimer was an instrument on which the player used small hammers with which to hit the strings, and it was thus the real ancestor of the piano.

These instruments and the secular songs of minstrels and mendicants are the foundations of our folk-music, both as it was sung and as it was danced. Its subjects are mainly those of peasants and farmers and freeholders. Husbandry in all its forms, hunting and poaching, eating and drinking, the ardours of the young and the wisdom of the old. Behind it all was the common guerdon of toil, the uncertainties of nature, and the ravages of war and disease, the scanty leisure, the rare feast, and the rough-and-ready games and pastimes which were all that ordinary men could know. The taverns both of town and country fostered and spread a communal gossip, a local wit and dialect, and these were often crystallized into songs and stories which endured for centuries.

2

When the permanent ascendancy of the Tudors at the end of the fifteenth century gave England a strong central government and a release from civil war, all these various relaxations began to settle down into cultivated and domestic arts. The private fortress was no longer so necessary and there grew up a gentler and more comfortable domestic architecture which could house a more refined and intimate manner of life. The lord's serf became the King's subject. The towns gained a considerable measure of wealth and freedom, and it was possible for the prosperous merchant to surround himself with many of the ornaments of leisure. The King's household was an elaborate organization of royal services, which included the amenities of the arts as well as the pomps of state. His Royal Chapel was a complete choir which travelled with him and provided ordered musical worship for the Court. He had his heralds and trumpeters, his household musicians; for feasts and diversions he could stage a play or a masque, and if his own tastes lay in any particular artistic direction he could exert great influence on its progress and repute. Both Henry VII and Henry VIII combined political strength of purpose with real sensitiveness to all the arts, and they gave music in particular a personal attention which was felt in every branch of cultivated society. The time was exactly ripe, for the new art of harmony which the Church had sponsored was ready to be transplanted into secular use, and the combination of this harmony with the rich vein of native lyric poetry produced a fine blossoming of social and domestic music of all kinds.

It was in Italy that the renaissance of the social arts first bore musical fruit. The Italian madrigal had been a rustic song, used in various dialects, and sung in two or three vocal parts as early as the fourteenth century. It became a very popular form of short lyric, written both by accomplished poets and by scores of amateur versifiers. As vocal polyphony became more complex in texture and more elastic in expression the madrigal followed it. It transferred to the secular practice of music all that harmony which the Church had developed, and it added a certain lightness and freedom of thought of its own. This madrigal form came to England.

Native speech gave it directness of expression, while secular surroundings encouraged a rhythmic lilt and movement more lively than the sacred settings of Biblical prose could bear. The educated Tudor household sang its madrigals, airs, and ballets, all vocal in origin, and all founded on the same harmonies and the same devices of imitation which the masses and motets of the Church had made familiar. The Airs were often like a formal song, with its regular rhymes and stanzas, furnished with a vocal accompaniment of simple harmonies. The Ballet borrowed dance-rhythms and usually had a 'fal, la, la' refrain.

The Madrigal, like the motet, treated all its voices as individuals. The parts are equal in interest and importance, and should a number of voices, able and willing to read a part, find themselves under the same roof at a convenient time, the madrigal offered a perfect medium for their use. This was precisely what happened in the cultivated houses of late Renaissance Italy and Tudor England. To be able to read and sing a musical part was the normal accomplishment of educated circles, from the King's household downwards. It was this practice which encouraged the composition and publication of an enormous collection of secular vocal music, combining lyric poetry of surpassing beauty with polyphonic music of equal distinction. Nowhere, either before or since, do we find music of a quality so even, and of a quantity so great. The madrigal had become thoroughly domesticated.

The Tudors not only sang their ballets and madrigals, they played them too. Elizabeth's household included trumpets, sackbuts, flutes, lutes, harps, virginals, and viols, not to mention singers, minstrels, instrument-makers and 'musition strangers', probably

Italian. It was the viols, precursors of violin and violoncello, which were perfectly adapted to sustained and
melodious music. They were instruments of delicate
tone, as flexible and as homogeneous as voices. Music
'apt for voices' was equally 'apt for viols'. There is
evidence that our Tudor family mixed the two. Some
parts might be sung while others were played, and they
no doubt frequently doubled voices and viols. It was
an ideal medium, and it produced an ideal musical
literature, for the casual company of singers and players;
and it is proof of a very high level of general musical
culture. It is not the music of the exceptional and professed artist. It is the art of a society, of a whole educated class, whose chosen recreation was of this fine
quality.

Old melody, native poetry, and new harmony made
a combination of marvellous artistic power, and in the
singer-lutenist they could be simultaneously controlled
by one hand and voice. The songs of the lutenists had
the musical rhythm, rhyme, and form which came from
the verses of the old ballad-singers. There was a wonderful field of lyric poetry to explore, in a language still
fresh and stimulating. The finger-board of the lute
enabled the player of skill to suggest even the most
daring of the new harmonies, and he also could give
more than a hint of the interplay of moving parts. The
strings were plucked and the tone transient, but this
was a merit, in that it set out the melody of the singer
in clear relief. Of all the arts which man has devised
there is none which can be more direct and more moving
in effect than a solo voice playing its own accompaniment. This was the art of John Dowland and the
lutenist-singers.

The virginals, like the related spinet, were in essence

a mechanical harp, the strings being plucked by a
keyboard mechanism. Of the various mechanical devices which have been applied to music the keyboard is
by far the most important. It immediately encouraged
and consolidated that harmonic aspect of music which
then and for a long future was to be in the main line of
progress. Hand and keyboard together are peculiarly
suited to the practice of harmony. The keyboard
would have been a mere curiosity before harmony was
developed, for melodic speed and agility could be obtained in many other ways. The keyboard took its
permanent and increasing place in European music
because harmony was already an essential ingredient in
our appreciation, and anything which made harmonic
experience easy was sure of a welcome. If such a
mechanism could be made of a compactness and convenience suitable for domestic use, then nothing could
well compete with it as a musical and household amenity.
Any one possessing a keyboard could produce all the old
chords and experiment with new ones. Once tuned, the
instrument remained in tune for some time and spared
the performer the trouble both of finding the notes by
ear and of keeping them true to pitch. And the speed
and elaboration of keyboard music was only limited by
the power of eyes and fingers to read and execute.

Musicians took a long time to realize all this, and
early domestic keyboard music, like early organ music,
is fluid and tentative in style. Much of it is clearly
borrowed from the music of voices. Some pieces, full
of scales and arpeggios, are experiments in the new
technique of finger exercises. There are a very large
number of ornamental variations on airs and folk-songs,
sometimes of a technical elaboration highly ingenious.
Composers were attracted by the new devices of the

keyboard as such, and wrote many long pieces which were intellectually clever rather than artistically convincing. The one group of possible forms which fitted the mechanism of the keys at once was the immense collection of dance tunes of all kinds, which had enlivened every social festivity since social music began. These tunes could be harmonized, varied, and embellished. They already had a symmetry of form and cadence. They could be loosely grouped to provide contrasts of speed and mood. So fruitful were these dances in suggesting ideas of development and harmonic balance, that there is no historical gap between these first suites of dances and the more highly organized sonatas and symphonies which later gave instrumental music its own classical repertory. Pavane and Galliard, Almand, Saraband, and Gigue, the country dance of the village green and the stately posturings of the Court ball, all alike were brought into the domain of pure music, and they became the staple food of the domestic spinet.

It is tempting to ask why a social and domestic art so widespread and so admirable should have grown and matured just when it did, and why it should afterwards have declined so rapidly. The beginning of the seventeenth century in England saw the publication of hundreds of madrigals, among which are many of the best that have ever been written. A generation later the whole style seems to have become old-fashioned, and a great many of its best products obsolete and forgotten. Instrumental music did not so greatly decrease, but its style changed, and the most accomplished remnants were not equal to that wonderful general level of talent which had been so remarkable under the Tudor ascendancy. Just as the cultured societies of Italy had

given music the same creative impulse and the same
artistic status as painting and literature, so in Eliza-
bethan England there seemed to be no limits to the
appreciation and encouragement of music, and of the
best music that could be devised. Practice and discrimination went hand in hand. The fact that the
Royal House itself was devoted to the arts must have
given the movement a special impetus, and it is significant that the Stuarts who followed were far less accomplished. But this influence would not of itself have
produced a well-nigh universal art had not the people
been in some way peculiarly ready to welcome it. The
achievements of Tudor music must be accounted part
of that great expansion of horizon which a new poetical
and intellectual language, new processes of thought,
and the clear consciousness of unexplored worlds,
material, spiritual, and artistic, had brought so vividly
before the minds of all men. Had our seventeenth
century been politically more stable, we might perhaps
have helped to advance the new fashions as ably as we
had mastered the old. But our most active minds took
a violently political bias, and in the civil and religious
quarrels which split society from top to bottom during
the course of the century, the cultivation of the arts
became perforce a secondary and intermittent activity.
It was difficult enough to solve the fundamental problems on which social continuity of any kind so perilously
hung. The graces of life had to be left comparatively
unattended.

The English Puritans were not averse to music.
Their greatest prophet, John Milton, is sufficient proof
of a continued and passionate desire to harmonize voice
and verse. But the Puritans distrusted the Church,
which was the depository of the past, and they con-

demned the Stage, which then claimed the future. Their contribution to music was a modest household practice, culminating occasionally in an allegory or masque, in which songs and dances were incidental. Milton exaggerates when he says of Henry Lawes:

> Harry, whose tuneful and well-measured song
> First taught our English music how to span
> Words with just note and accent . . .

Lawes was a long way behind the Tudors, both in inspiration and method. Milton's lines show how distant and forgotten the Tudor arts had become. Yet there was certainly in Puritan England a good deal of attractive music which both satisfied good taste and filled the demands of Puritan leisure.

With the Restoration came new fashions from France. Purcell had to work largely in tune with them, but he was too big to fit into any precise mould. His songs have a freedom, a pathos, and a beauty which no composer of his time, English or foreign, could approach. His music for strings leaned towards the new, but kept much of the solidity of the old. His keyboard music, though neither so prophetic as that of Germany, nor so neat as that of France, yet had its own sturdy freshness. Some of his instrumental chamber sonatas are not likely to fade. And there were hundreds of devoted amateurs, like Pepys with his flute, who lost no chance of hearing and playing any of this domestic music, native or imported, which came within their taste and competence.

3

The most firmly entrenched society in seventeenth-century Europe was that of France, so far as the Court and its amenities were concerned. Government was already highly centralized when the young king Louis XIV began to surround himself with every embellishment which power and wealth could conceive. His flair for men of distinction and his success in attracting them to his place and person earned for his reign the title of *le grand siècle*, and for several subsequent generations every princeling in Europe was to some degree his imitator. The less attractive sides of the picture, the increasing penury of the peasants, the fatal wars of aggrandizement, and the fashions of royal extravagance which sowed the seeds of ultimate bankruptcy and revolution in the next century, were not under Louis so obvious as the undisputed triumphs of the taste and patronage which he lavished on all the arts then current. His success was beyond argument, and though the scope of any form of patronage must necessarily depend on the prevailing moods of the patron, Louis XIV certainly covered a very wide field. Naturally, the arts he encouraged were those which could best reflect the views of himself and his court, but within these limits he found room for a very remarkable assembly of men of talent. His soldiers, statesmen, financiers, architects, engineers, poets, dramatists, and painters would make a list of extraordinary distinction. His musicians were no less talented and no less favoured. Even his cooks were men of European repute.

Elaborate formality, strict etiquette, and a precise care for the niceties of speech and manners are the natural consequence of living under a prince with 'divine' rights. Louis was pleased to assume the title of the sun, and his planets, major and minor, had to move around him with becoming deference. The arts he fostered were concerned not so much with broad human values as with the tasteful and ornamental expression of aristocratic leisure. His public works were sumptuous and imposing. His recreations were lavish in expense, but carefully detailed and proportioned. Music of an intimate type had to conform to the artificial behaviour of the royal presence, to the courtesies of a strictly regulated familiarity. Charming songs about shepherds and shepherdesses had little to do with the smell of the earth, or with the real risks and toils of crude nature. They reflected the courtly pastime of pretending to be countrified, of dabbling gracefully in the more pleasant pursuits of farm and dairy, of tending intermittently a carefully selected and well-protected garden. Fountains and lakes were made to appear where they would most effectively strike the attention. Hedges and avenues were cut to what seemed to be a desirable pattern. Nature was pruned of its wayward manners and made into an ordered and formal spectacle. Wild flowers were not encouraged. A later wit has written of the cult of the 'week-end' cow, and there is a certain similarity between some of our modern incursions into nature and these pastoral caperings of the French court. Delightful they are, these old French songs of well-groomed landscapes and decorous peasants. Their neatness of form, aptness of ornament, and precise command of just those accents and inflexions which suggest a delicate emotion, leave a very pleasant taste. There are no depths of passion, but there are also no crudities.

The same atmosphere envelops the parallel art of the French clavecinists. Spinet, clavecin, cembalo, and harpsichord are different names for what was in essentials the same instrument. This domestic keyboard fitted admirably into the French salon, and a succession of sensitive players and composers raised it

into one of the most accomplished departments of
French music. The famous family of the Couperins
provides an example of the gifts and circumstances
which have so often culminated in permanent and outstanding musical achievements. There was a long
family tradition of music, an aristocratic society highly
appreciative of this talent, and an instrument admirably
suited to display both the imagination of the composer
and player, and the delicate taste of the listener.
Neither violent emotion nor abstruse thought would
have been in keeping with the aesthetic fashions of the
time. Graceful melody, delicate ornament, neat form,
and the fancies of a lively but restrained emotion were
the desirable gifts, and the most distinguished of the
Couperins, François, had these talents in command
beyond all his contemporaries. Life in a society of
delicate discrimination made the pieces of Couperin not
unlike the pictures of Watteau. They are like the most
exquisite of the costumes and furnishings of Versailles.
The fine embroidery of trills and grace-notes with
which Couperin decorates his melodies are like the
ruffles of fine lace, like the sparkling beads of a lustre.
'*Il faut tout sacrifier*,' he wrote, '*au goût à la propreté des
passages et à bien attendrir les accens marqués par les
pincés.*' His whimsical titles are distinguished by the
same delicate choice. His reapers dance lightly, his
knitting-girls chatter gaily, his nun is sweetly demure.
There is sometimes a hint of pathos, a suggestion of
mystery, but always subdued, always disciplined by the
canons of a perfect sense of fitness. François Couperin
was a very gifted artist. Within his small range he is
incomparable. He influenced other composers who
were poles removed from his environment, some of
them men of far greater stature than himself. This

influence was always in the direction of beauty and clarity. His music is of the salon, and it is the salon of a refined and conscious elegance. The traditions of this art have survived through two centuries of French music. There have always been in France, as there still are, players and composers intimately akin in spirit to the work and ideals of Couperin.

Any one interested in the effect of social contrasts on the products of an art could hardly find a more illuminating example than is afforded by a comparison between the work of the Couperin family in France and that of the Bach family in Germany. John Sebastian Bach was about twenty years junior to Couperin. Both men were the apex of a family and social tradition which long preceded and long survived them. Both embodied points of view and methods of expression which were essential parts of their respective surroundings. It is very doubtful if Couperin knew anything of the Bachs. Germany was not then a model to France, as France was a model to Germany. Bach certainly studied Couperin, and confessed the fact in some of his smaller pieces.

German clavier-music tells a very different story from that of France. It begins by being very near to the organ. The more instrumental style which the great north-German organists had adopted with such intellectual thoughtfulness and dignity was often transferred to the clavier. There was one keyboard instrument favoured in some German circles which did not belong to the harpsichord family. This was the clavichord, for which Bach wrote much. Its strings were pressed, and could be made to give detailed variations of tone. But the instrument was exceedingly quiet and delicate, hardly audible in a large room or in combination with other instruments, and the keyboards most common in Germany were, like those of England, France, and Italy, members of the harpsichord family, which plucked the strings and had an even but incisive tone. Clavier is loosely used as a general term for all keyboards. They played at first preludes and fugues of the simpler type, dances like the chaconne, variations on folk-song and Chorale. There was much whimsical experiment, much bald imitation. Compared with the cultured perfection of France, the German school is clumsy and formless.

But long before Bach there is already a depth and daring in it which will ultimately feed the imagination of the future. The folk-songs are of the patient, long-suffering peasantry. Some of them have passed through the thirty years of war and famine with which the seventeenth century began. The Chorales are in themselves a religion. The organ already has its associations of faith and freedom. It is possible to put into the melodic fragment of a fugue subject such a concentration of thought and expression as will survive the wear and tear of a long contrapuntal development. Such mental exercises demand intense and sustained effort. When they fail they fail completely. There is no easy formula of rhymes and stanzas that will make a moderate talent appear at least clear and competent. North Germany remained for a long time remote from the fashions which had already conquered Italy and France. Southern Europe had pronounced itself emphatically in favour of formal melody and harmonic structure while the northern organists were still battling with polyphony of severely intellectual texture. Even when the Germans took a simple melody and wrote variations on it, most of their experiments were in the direction of complicated part-writing. In this process they discovered many beauties unknown to the more facile music of the south, but it was not an art that could possibly appeal to those who looked for soothing ditties or for easily digested form. To those of us who have since learnt to follow the thoughts of Bach and Handel, these their earlier models are full of prophetic suggestions of which we know the ultimate value. But to contemporary opinion in France and Italy a great deal of the music of Germany must have seemed as uncouth and forbidding as German speech and manners.

Germany in fact remained for a long time as hopelessly old-fashioned in art as she was in politics. Her religious reforms were the one and only revolution in her State. Her whole social system belonged to the Middle Ages. Till the end of the eighteenth century Germany was a conglomeration of nearly three hundred separate governments and principalities, each with its own local laws, tolls, customs, money, weights, and measures. And there was hardly a tolerable road in the whole realm. There were scores of small and virtually self-contained societies in which intense local feeling and general lack of intercourse with the outside world combined to preserve ideals and manners already centuries behind the times. The German peasant was a serf in the strict sense long after many of his peasant contemporaries elsewhere had won a large measure of freedom. The guilds and petty hierarchies of the Middle Ages were still prevalent and powerful. That the arts of Germany should therefore bear unmistakable traits of the past was but a natural consequence of the prevailing social backwardness. And if at the beginning of the eighteenth century there was to be found in Europe a man whose artistic conservatism was a match for these medieval survivals, that man was John Sebastian Bach.

With respect to the normal cosmopolitan taste of his time, Bach's music was out of date before it was written. Even in Germany the discoveries of Italy and France were not altogether unknown. There were many provincial courts which tried to follow the newer fashions, and many musicians who served them as best they could. Kuhnau, Bach's predecessor at Leipzig, out-Heroded Herod in his bold adoption of the dramatic ideas which came first from Italy. His sonatas have hardly a parallel until we reach the symphonic poems of the nineteenth century. He wrote Biblical stories on the keyboard, purely descriptive in aim, remarkably original in matter, and dramatic beyond anything which pure music had yet attempted. This was the man whom Bach succeeded. To turn from Kuhnau's pages to those of Bach is to jump back a century. Apart altogether from his purely musical gifts, Bach must have had a character of amazing strength. He looked towards the past, he embraced everything in it that he found congenial, he pursued its ideals to the limit of his powers, and he never wavered.

Bach was a fine organist, but there was nothing unusual in that. All the Bachs, for generations, had been leading musicians wherever they lived. Sebastian had a phenomenal mastery of the sheer science of composition. In this he outstripped the best. But his repute was local, he had no influence whatever on European taste, and very little in Germany itself. Such powers as he had were chiefly known through his sons and pupils, and even they felt towards him much as did the few outsiders who came in contact with his work. He was what the eighteenth century called an ingenious composer, rather than an inspired one. No one could dispute his amazing technique, but his methods were already academic, valuable no doubt as a severe training, but far too complex and intellectual to appeal to ordinary ears. A whole library of his music, which is now the staple fare of our best interpretative talent, was in his own day really obsolete, except as a peculiarly exacting form of musical education. It was almost a family affair. Perhaps that was the secret of its abiding strength; for of all the household music which has ever been written that of the Bach family in Leipzig is the most astonishing.

There was Anna Magdalena's book, and the Little Preludes and Inventions. There was the fine recreation of forty-eight Preludes and Fugues in all keys, major and minor, two each. There were French Suites and English Suites and Partitas, the great detached Sonatas, the violin sonatas, the flute sonatas, the violoncello sonatas. Hundreds of movements of every kind were there for this extraordinary company of children, pupils, and friends. And the creator of it all would never for a bar forget his supreme discipline of thought, his unapproachable technical dexterity. This music was more difficult to play, more exacting to think, and more conservative in feeling than any music then in existence. Such was the daily fare of the Bach circle. One would give a great deal to have a glimpse into that unique workshop. There were two centuries of tradition behind it, and a present genius which knew no limits.

Around it was Bach's more public work, his Passions and his three hundred and fifty Church Cantatas. There were volumes of organ music, the best ever written, and concertos for almost every possible combina-

tion of instruments. Nor did this incredible fertility
exhaust him. He copied everything striking which
came his way, a great deal of Italian music, even one
work by Purcell. Bach was a provincial, and nowhere
at that time were there any printed stores of music to
draw upon. The nearest modern equivalent of his lot
would be that of a cathedral organist who had to provide,
by his own hand, all the music which a whole society,
incessantly busy singing and playing, could devour,
both publicly and privately. Bach did this, and had
time to spare, for he also mended and invented instruments. It is a story of marvellous energy, vitality, and
craftsmanship, and it would be unthinkable in that
superficial world which merely pursues a public fame.
Intense local and family tradition brought every young
Bach into the world a musician born, and then set him
a unique standard of education. John Sebastian was its
summit, and the works he wrote for his family and
pupils have been very near the height of every performer's ambition since. Beethoven first impressed the
élite of Vienna by his understanding and performance
of Bach. Every subsequent aspirant to the first rank
has had to do the same, or confess his limitations. Such
was the domestic music of Bach's house in the eighteenth
century. Old-fashioned it was indeed, but after a
manner so consummate that every other fashion seems
by comparison fluid and transitory. That little family
circle has grown until it now covers the whole exalted
world of music.

Handel's harpsichord Lessons and Suites differ from
those of Bach in two respects. He had been to Italy and
had played with Domenico Scarlatti, and his use of the
keyboard is freer than Bach's scrupulous part-writing
would normally permit. Handel's interests were public

and cosmopolitan, but he had a solid German temperament and training when he cared to use them. The contrast between him and Bach is rather a contrast of character. Bach is more intimate, more intellectual, more introspective, and his craftsmanship is fastidious. Handel is direct, objective, breezy, almost casual. But for solid acceptance of broad values, for fine fresh verve, for pathos without sentiment, Handel has his own undisputed realm. His smaller works have been neglected, by comparison with his choral masterpieces. They are no less characteristic, and no less satisfying.

4

And now we must turn to Italy and inquire more precisely what constituted those new musical paths which were held to be so great an advance on the past, and which made the conservative instincts of Bach appear to look backward rather than forward. What was this Italian ascendancy which made its very language the universal speech of music? It is a fact which strikes every beginner in the art, whether performer or reader, that all our common musical terms are Italian. The great categories, Opera, Oratorio, Concerto, and the like, the general indications of speed and tone, and a host of detailed marks of expression and interpretation, are all Italian, and are found in the music of every composer, of every nationality. Even those fervid patriots who have insisted on putting every term they could into a native equivalent have not been able to abolish *forte* or *piano*, *crescendo*, *diminuendo*, and the common signs and abbreviations of Italian origin. Music is in this respect an Italian art, and the repute which gave all these words their world-wide currency can have been of no ordinary stamp.

All Italy's contributions to the musical history of the seventeenth and eighteenth centuries, and they were both great and various, had as their main ingredient the exceptional skill of the solo performer. This was her chief discovery. She found and used the marvellous artistic power of the single voice, of the single hand. This was also the real break with the past. Music had hitherto been, in its highest forms, a concerted art, an essentially corporate activity in which all performers were of equal artistic rank, however varied they might be in function. Italy began to select and train the individual exceptionally gifted, and her name for him, the *virtuoso*, is still with us. For this able, expert, courageous, forthright talent (*virtuoso* is untranslatable) she provided an organized training and a special music. She took her voices young, and by natural flair and hard discipline she brought them to such a pitch of efficiency that they became unquestionably the most perfect instruments of music then existing. They could sustain their tone, they could vary it, they could trill and repeat and leap with a melodic power and accuracy never before known. They established universal standards, *bel canto*, *cantilena*, *coloratura*. Instinctively the music they required was melody, melody for all purposes and at all costs. Harmony was a background by comparison, a modest frame from which the vocal line could effectively stand out. Complicated part-writing was sheer distraction, a waste of effort. It soon became a scholarly anachronism. The singer wanted to sing, and the listeners wanted to hear him clearly. All else was a means to that end.

The time was remarkably favourable. The keyboard had made simple harmonies so easy to play that there was no need even to write them. Given a tune and a

bass, the competent accompanist could provide harmonies at sight. This is the origin of the figured or
thorough-bass, as it was called. It was not an academic
exercise, but a universal practice amongst all trained
players of organ or harpsichord. With ready mind and
fingers, differing only in degree of resource, they were
ready to harmonize anything, just as the modern school-
boy 'vamps'. The result was ample for its purpose,
and a very great saving of time and labour. This
practice of filling-in the harmonies at sight, on the
organ or harpsichord, survived and sufficed for nearly
two centuries of music, and for the most distinguished
as well as for the most unpretentious forms.

Melody being of prime importance, then phrasing
and design must be melodically evolved. There were
already hundreds of old songs which offered simple
models, but these expert singers wanted much more
than that. There must be scales and pauses, shakes and
ornaments, that would properly display the trained
voice. Moreover, there must be subject-matter that
would give opportunities for showing personal or
histrionic emotions, both grave and gay. The quality
of the words as poetry mattered little. They must
describe a suitable situation and be easy to vocalize.
The versifiers worked to this formula as readily as the
accompanists did to the figured bass. What was wanted
was a vocal music as suitable for small occasions as the
great operatic scenes were for more public use. Italy
solved this problem by the solo cantata, a form now
obsolete, but in its time a very popular means of semi-
private music-making. The subject was usually a
dramatic scene or incident, the interpreter a highly expert solo voice. In the simpler examples the only written
accompaniment was a bass. Lully took the method and

applied it to his French scenes and dialogues, whence
it reached England in Purcell's time. Some of Purcell's
more elaborate songs show decided traces of these
origins. So, on a higher spiritual plane, do the solo cantatas of Bach. The Italian solo cantata was a neat solution of a new problem. Singers were becoming more
and more individual and professional. Cultured musical
circles naturally wished to be closely associated with
them. The solo cantata provided an appropriate link.

The solo-player was also in demand, though for
some time he was, as a specialist, far less advanced than
the singer. The keyboard was in constant use, the old
dance-forms were enriched by development, and a
great many more specifically virtuoso-pieces were
written. The keyboard was peculiarly suited for extemporizing. Accompaniment was largely extempore
in any case, but solo extemporizing also had its accepted
place in all friendly music-making. It was an obvious
field for rivalry, and it soon became an indispensable
accomplishment in all players of repute. The famous
competition between Domenico Scarlatti and Handel
was a contest in improvisation. Less gifted men must
have indulged in a good deal of commonplace meander-
ing and conventional fireworks, but every one learnt to
use the keyboard freely, and to discover the style of
music for which it was best adapted. The young Scarlatti was undoubtedly the most emancipated of them
all. His style, both of playing and writing, was that of
a specialist. He used the harpsichord, not as an instrument for reproducing other kinds of music, but as a
means of expression individual and complete in itself.
Compared with his contemporaries, Bach and Handel,
his technique is remarkably modern. He believed, as
he put it, in using all his ten fingers. He also learnt to

leap about on the instrument in a way which was at
that time as novel as it was effective. His art is that of
the solo-performer who specializes in the peculiar
resources of a chosen instrument. As he also had a
delightful musical fancy, his pieces have remained
perennially fresh and engaging. They have been the
delight of all players who were attracted by skilled
precision and clarity of thought.

But though the singers of Italy were unrivalled, and
her harpsichord players among the best, there was yet
another field in which she outshone all competitors,
and made contributions to music of supreme value.
Italy's greatest discovery, in ultimate power and fertility, was the art of the violin. She virtually created
the instrument, and she produced a succession of
composers and performers whose genius evolved the
style on which all subsequent masterpieces of chamber
and orchestral music have been built. The small town
of Cremona is a household word among musicians
because there her craftsmen turned the delicate little
viol into the brilliant violin. They produced an instrument which for power, variety, and beauty could con-
fidently challenge even a superbly trained voice. And
its range was far greater. It could play the melodies
which everybody loved almost as well as a singer could
sing them, and it could also do a great many things far
beyond the capacity of any voice. The possibilities of
the violin were not all discovered at once. Generations
of players each added their portion to its special technique. But it was clear from the first that no other
instrument had such powers of melodic expression, and
this faculty was precisely in keeping with the general
taste of the time. Moreover, violin, viola, and violoncello could be used in the same intimate way as the

older viols had been used. What we now call classical chamber music is founded on the quartet of strings, two violins, one viola, and one violoncello. It is the transfer of the traditional quartet of voices, soprano, contralto, tenor, and bass, to instruments of comparable melodic quality.

The founder of the great Italian school of violin-playing was Arcangelo Corelli, a contemporary of the most famous of the Cremona craftsmen, Stradivarius, who worked in the latter part of the seventeenth century. The singers had their special *cantata*, a word which means something sung. Corelli wrote for his violins a *suonata*, which means something played. That is how the word sonata came into music. Its more special significance in musical form is a later growth. Corelli's sonatas were mostly written for two violins and a violoncello, with or without a harpsichord, which added harmonies. 'Suonate da camera' he called them, chamber-sonatas, and with these works a golden period of intimate domestic music begins. Corelli's new style was of great refinement and beauty. He could write contrasted movements which yet kept a unity of atmosphere. His workmanship was invariably scholarly, and he set a standard of instrumental sensitiveness which is still the hall-mark of all good chamber-music. It was the pursuit of an art comparable to that of the best madrigal-writing, in which each performer gave an individual and equal share to the combined effect. It appealed especially to the more discriminating tastes, of players and listeners alike, and it put pure instrumental music, in its own sphere and of its own right, on a plane equal to that of the best vocal music of the past. It is significant that Corelli is the first composer whose work is exclusively instrumental. He stands on a great dividing line. Before him all the masterpieces of music employed voices. After him come the triumphs of sonata, quartet, concerto, and symphony.

For those who wished to play or hear a particular instrument, the solo sonata offered exactly the right medium. For those whose delight was in combinations of equal performers, there was scope for endless variety. It was even possible to employ a number of players of very varied powers. This was the genesis of those early concertos in which one or two solo performers are supported by a 'chorus' of players less skilled. The households of the best patrons of music began to be organized in this fashion, a quite momentous development. The concertos of Corelli, like those of Bach and Handel, are half-way between chamber music and concert music. The aristocratic patron himself, his friends and servants, could take a modest part at one of the desks of the accompanying strings, while the expert performers could play the more exacting solo parts. It was this custom, a very frequent one, which encouraged the growing taste for concertos, and indirectly for the later symphonies.

The eighteenth century is a curious period in our musical history. Public taste was in certain respects of a very inferior order. It was the age of some of the shallowest forms of music, pretentious in method and barren in thought, which have ever entered the Church or occupied the Stage. Yet there were, scattered about Europe, many palaces and many town and country houses where concerted music of a very distinguished kind was a regular feature of the leisured hour. Of all the music which has yet been evolved, the string quartet, for example, is within the highest categories. The demands it makes both on players and listeners are

of skilled nicety and judgement. It is music for the
intimate and educated circle, whether amateur or professional. It flourishes where standards are most exacting, and nowhere else. This was the taste which the
best patrons of the eighteenth century so signally
fostered. It was essentially an aristocratic art, both
socially and aesthetically, but it alone made possible
that wider society which could eventually find a niche
for the chamber-music of Haydn, Mozart, Beethoven,
Schubert, and Brahms, each in his turn. The impetus
given by these first patrons became in time so extended
that in certain parts of Europe, Germany being in the
end the most fruitful soil of all, an unmusical household
was almost unknown.

Instrumental chamber-music was not of course confined to strings. There was Frederick the Great and
his flute. Frederick deserves generous mention in the
story of music because he combined so remarkably
the soldier, the statesman, and the artist. He showed
the whole world that it was not merely possible, but
a genuine mark of the balanced character, to be at the
same time formidable in war, astute in council, and
creative in art. He interfered directly in matters of
education, instituting regular singing-lessons in the
schools 'By His Majesty's Command', and he set an
example of practical musicianship which had no small
effect on his countrymen and contemporaries. The
almost superstitious reverence for 'old Fritz', the hero
of a great war and the maker of a great power, was
extended to his hobbies as well as to his triumphs in
battle and diplomacy. He had practised music in
defiance of his father, and as soon as he had the liberty
to do so he put into it the same energy, will, and precision which marked all his exploits. He chose servants

who could play, and practised duets with his valet. His
daily concert was as regularly organized as the parade
of his Guards. No distinguished musician was allowed
to come near him without a welcome and a part to play.
He had strong likes and dislikes, but what he liked he
liked permanently, and set no bounds to its cultivation.
Concerted music, with his own flute in it, was his
passion.

Frederick was notably faithful and generous to his
teacher Quantz, who wrote some three hundred concertos for the flute, which Frederick preferred above
all other compositions of the kind. These concertos
the king played daily, and in a regular sequence. He
was a complete autocrat in this as in other spheres.
He decided what was to be played and would set out the
parts himself, and in his own solos he took liberties
with the time and interpretation which his accompanist
frequently found somewhat disconcerting. This accompanist was for many years Bach's most famous son,
Carl Philipp Emanuel, whom Frederick had appointed
at his accession. They were not always musically in
sympathy, but the king had a very great respect for
Carl's talent and traditions, and it was due to this
personal link that there occurred the oft-recorded visit of
old John Sebastian himself to Potsdam in 1747. When
Frederick found Bach's name in the list of arrivals he
announced it at once to his suite: 'Gentlemen, old
Bach has come,' and insisted on an immediate audience,
before the traveller had even time to change his coat.
Frederick stopped his concert, showed Bach his collection of instruments, heard with delight Bach's
improvisations, and asked him for a fugue in six parts.
Using a theme given to him by Frederick, Bach afterwards wrote his 'Musical Offering', dedicated to 'a

sovereign admired in music as in all other sciences of
war and peace'. The meeting between these two remarkable characters is a vivid moment in the story of
music.

Not that either Frederick or any other contemporary
ever realized the stature of the elder Bach as we now
see it. The most enlightened opinion of the time held
that Carl Philipp Emanuel far outstripped his father,
and so far as the general trend of taste was concerned,
this was undoubtedly true. Carl wrote and published
the first comprehensive text-book of keyboard technique,
a work which immediately gave him a foremost influence. He had originality and imagination of a very high
order, and his harpsichord sonatas were the acknowledged models of Haydn, Mozart, and Beethoven. He
it was who did most to lay down the accepted principles of harmonic design on an extended scale. The
contrapuntal method, of which his father was the finest
exponent, had built extended movements by developing
a rich and varied texture. Carl belonged to the later
school of more formal themes attached to a plan of
contrasted harmonic sections. He excelled in a balanced
sense of design and in appropriate modulations. There
is in him at times a concentration of mood not unworthy
to foreshadow the maturity of Beethoven. His works
are now forgotten, but they were accepted universally
as the greatest single contribution to the evolution of
the sonata, and thus to a whole category of extended
instrumental forms. It was this originality which Dr.
Burney had in mind when he wrote, on meeting Carl
and comparing his sonatas with his father's fugues,
that the work of the son so clearly excelled that of
the father. This opinion sounds strange to-day, but it
was shared by all the most sensitive musicians of the

later eighteenth century. It is a warning example of the pitfalls which beset even the best contemporary judgement.

Carl's best pupil was Joseph Haydn, though the two men never met. Haydn mastered the new designs and added to them the resources of his own surroundings and the warmth of his own personality. The two Haydn brothers, Joseph and Michael, are informing examples of the effects of patronage as it was practised in the eighteenth century. Michael, hardly less gifted than his brother, was condemned to spend his talents on the barren fashions of church music, as it was then understood by a powerful and insensitive Archbishop of Salzburg. Joseph had the good fortune to find himself in the household of the Princes Esterhazy, whose taste was exemplary. These princes, like the great Frederick, made music the channel of their artistic life, and thirty years in their service made Joseph Haydn into one of the guiding spirits of European music. The eighty-three string quartets of Haydn are as fine a tribute to his patrons as they are to his own genius. They could never have been written without a direct and personal encouragement of the purest type. They have been the delight of countless players, of every class and standard, who wished to make music in their own homes or in the select company of congenial minds. They placed the string quartet permanently among the classic forms, and they fed the taste on which all later examples have been built. Haydn had an unremitting liveliness of thought, a homely wit, unfailing craftsmanship, and an exact knowledge of the characteristic beauties of his instruments. The Croatian peasant gave him folk-songs and folk-dances which he could use as the material and model of his own ready inventions. There is a warmth

in these themes and melodies which keeps them as fresh
and fragrant to-day as they were when he wrote them
a century and a half ago. His chief asset, though he
often chafed at it, was the combined fitness and permanence of his post, and the comparative seclusion
which allowed him to unfold with steady purpose a
character as complete and satisfying in its range as was
that of the elder Bach in his. Haydn never ceased to be
the servant of his prince, he had to sit 'below the salt',
but that prince supplied musical resources which Haydn
was able to count on permanently, day after day and
year after year, and it is not too much to say that he and
his master together literally created the most characteristic form in all chamber-music. Our home and halls
alike enjoy the heritage of this music, which Prince
Nicholas Esterhazy liked, and which Joseph Haydn
wrote under his roof.

   Mozart, Beethoven, and Schubert in due time followed the path which Haydn had so clearly defined. In
the Austrian Empire, and particularly in Vienna, the
place of instrumental chamber-music became comparable to the vogue of the madrigal in Tudor England. Like
the madrigal, it could count on the highest social approval and practice. The Archduke Rudolf, Waldstein,
Rasoumovsky, and scores of other noble patrons were
men who knew music from the inside, whose taste was
formed by the combined influences of practical musicianship and close association with the most gifted and
creative minds. It was not a merely material generosity,
it was a direct and personal devotion to the art. It
attracted to Vienna every musician of standing. It
radiated from Vienna the classical chamber-music of
the whole world.

G

5

Haydn was an old man, Beethoven a young one, when the pianoforte first began to supersede the harpsichord in public favour. The change is significant. The piano had existed in the elder Bach's time. Frederick the Great had a fine collection and showed Bach the best models. Bach was not converted, nor were players in general attracted by the instrument. Yet the harpsichord, with its unvarying tone, its poor sustaining power, and its total lack of detailed contrast, seems to us a very much narrower means of expression than even a moderately efficient piano. Large harpsichords had two manuals, and a provision of differing jacks and strings which gave general changes of tone. There were octave couplers which added brilliance, and some of the best models had a shuttered sound-box controlled by a pedal, thus giving a broad crescendo. But all these devices affected a whole row of keys at once. Nothing could be done to mark a single note, or bring out an inside part, or vary the comparative loudness of the notes in a chord. Natural conservatism made the early pianos imitate the harpsichord somewhat closely in actual tone-quality. The hammers were hard, the strings thin, and the tone was much more metallic and much less sustained that we are now accustomed to. The direct power of the finger, however, was there, with all its easy control of detailed variety. To a modern pianist an early piano is very limited in range and quality of tone, but the harpsichord is more limited still. It feels curiously remote. A clean blow on the key is all the player can do. Gradations of touch have no effect whatever. It follows therefore that 'expression', as we commonly use the term, did not exist on the harpsichord; all the player could really control was speed. He had no detailed mastery either of quantity or quality of sound. Why did the eighteenth century hesitate to adopt the piano, which gave the player so direct a command of both?

There are two answers to this question. The harpsichord was to be found everywhere, the standard of manufacture was high, and artists are affected no less than other men by use and wont. They preferred the instrument they knew. But there was a second reason which goes much deeper into the aesthetic taste of the time. Players in general simply did not feel the need for devices of expression on the keyboard as we know them. A good harpsichord was clear, incisive, brilliant. It was very effective in speed of articulation and in elaborate melodic ornament. The eighteenth century wanted no more. There was then no conception of the suggestiveness of tone-variation in detail as we practise it; the intimate relation of the single finger with the actual blow on the string was outside the consciousness both of the harpsichord player and of his music. It was therefore outside his notions of what was desirable. The eighteenth century invented the piano, but it was the nineteenth which adopted it.

And here too there were deep causes. The nineteenth century was the era of a new romanticism, of personal values, of democratic ardour, of individual and social emancipation. Anything which offered a personal and direct means of expression was in tune with the age. Beethoven used the piano as a vivid personal channel of thought, with every subtlety and emphasis of utterance. Many of his conservative contemporaries felt that more reticence would have improved him. He played with a naked fervour which was at times almost musical bad manners. He made what appeared to be a deliberate exhibition of his emotions. There was a Byronic side to Beethoven, in some of his moods, which the eighteenth century would not easily have tolerated, but which the piano encouraged him to express. One can expound, one can preach, one can rant on the piano. It has the power, as it also has the extravagance, of romantic poetry. The harpsichord is narrower, but it is also less explosive.

Further, the piano can, to those who are sensitive, suggest many other kinds of music. It can even give a hint of orchestral colour. It can imitate a pizzicato, or smash its chords like a brass band. It can mark a melody, and it can cover the whole texture of its harmony with a vibrating haze of sustaining pedal. It would be hard to 'arrange' the symphonies of Beethoven for the harpsichord. His whole dynamic system would be lost. One can arrange them for the piano, and give more than a hint of the original score in the process. The tone of the piano is limited in quality, but its variations of quantity are infinite, and it has gone on steadily adding to its power and to its emotional range. The sonatas of Beethoven have a personal and detailed eloquence quite outside the view of the harpsichord. Beethoven, before the advent of the piano, would have been, in this field, another and quite different composer.

These new powers of direct expression, and the music which developed them, were so congenial in spirit to the general outlook of the new era that the piano rapidly became extraordinarily popular. Its command, under one pair of hands, of independent and contrasted strands of thought made it able to compete with the concerted music of other instruments, and this was indirectly a serious loss to music as a corporate art.

But the piano also reached thousands of houses which might otherwise have remained musically silent, and this was a great gain. Social revolution was creating a large new middle class, whose homes and incomes, though small in comparison with those of some of the former patrons of music, yet provided a standard of comfort and leisure sufficient for many of the simpler artistic pursuits. For these homes the piano was ideal. A competent player could cover an enormous musical literature. The piano could accompany, it could reproduce the orchestral and vocal music of symphony, opera, and oratorio, it had all the harpsichord music of the past to choose from, and a rapidly accumulating library of its own. It came, like so many other amenities of life, under the influence of the industrial revolution. It was constant in improvement and was reproduced in hundreds of thousands. In the cottage model it became as familiar to the peasant and artisan as its predecessors had ever been to the more leisured classes.

There is no need to catalogue the library of the domestic pianist. His especial classics are the sonatas of Beethoven. There in fullest measure are to be found beauty and truth, joy, tragedy, and humour, the call of romance, the charm of fantasy, all expressed with the sincerity and candour of a unique genius. It is recorded how difficult Beethoven could be in the normal intercourse of men, how unaccountable in mood, how violent in expression. He would not play if certain people were in the room. It was never sure that he would play at all. But once coaxed to the piano, or taken there by his own whim, he would extemporize for an hour on end, charming, exciting, melting, at times almost frightening his friends by the passionate fervour of his creative fancy. He was as a man possessed, completely absorbed in the adventures of his own spirit, and he carried with him the minds of his hearers, until they too forgot the march of time and the tasks of ordinary life. This intensity and this stark honesty is plainly found in his written music, and it is often expressed in terms so simple that a player of average attainment can come within reach of it. Nothing has done more to bring vivid musical experience within the ambit of a simple culture than this personal eloquence of Beethoven at the piano. He has never disappointed the sturdy faith of the amateur, however clumsy and uncertain of finger, that within his pages was to be found an art worth striving after. He has given the humble home of the working man and woman a vision and an artistic status beyond that of many places of far greater pretension. He led the way for Chopin and Schumann, though in these the technique of playing is often so highly specialized that the amateur is at great straits to do it justice. They are not really more difficult than Beethoven, but they have not his frequent moods of grand simplicity. Mendelssohn was nearer to him in finger technique.

Taste has a way of progressing backwards. From Beethoven men turn to Mozart, with his delicate and refreshing clarity, his grace and precision, his controlled emotion, as of the harpsichord. Lately the tide has flowed strongly in the direction of the still earlier eighteenth century, and particularly towards Bach. We are learning to enjoy that solid fare of lively counterpoint which used to be left to specialists, and rather academic ones at that. We are beginning to realize that something well worth saying and repeating can be put into a two-part invention, while a fugue can be as exciting and as vivid as a symphony. Technical fashions are in the long run as nothing, compared with the quality of the thought which makes them live. The piano no doubt puts into these old works a great deal of tonal detail which their composers never imagined, but that is precisely the attraction, as it is also the danger, of the piano. It can do anything. It can work with all the older partners in chamber music, and it can accompany a voice far better than any other single instrument. The songs of the nineteenth century, no less than its sonatas, are founded on the special resources of the piano.

When social and political ferment found a voice in romantic and nature-loving poetry, in a wide emotional and intellectual horizon, and in a warm interest in the desires and fortunes of whole classes of men hitherto obscure and powerless, there arose with it an intimate art of song of very high quality. The works of Schubert were the fine fruits of the movement. They gave the solo voice and its accompanying piano a status not inferior to the best quartets and symphonies. Schumann and Brahms in turn followed this same ideal, and there were few composers of distinction who did not add something to its harvest. The combination of romantic or dramatic lyrics with a melody redolent of the loveliest inflexions of folk-song, the whole suffused and enhanced by the infinite suggestiveness of the piano, produced an artistic medium as fertile as imagination could wish. It was predominantly a German art, in words and melody as in rich sobriety of illustration and atmosphere. It sang of hills and dales, of fields and woods, of peasants and millers and poetic wanderers, of their desires and affections, their haunts and homes. It was an art of the hearth, of the fragrant countryside. It bespeaks an interest in homely things, a share of life's tasks and comforts, and an occasional hour of leisure when emotions may be garnered in tranquillity. We sing these songs in our concert-halls, but they are not properly at home there. They, like the most intimate forms of chamber music, of which they are a newer vocal counterpart, were written for the music-room, for places where there is no real barrier between performers and listeners, where the appreciation of music and the making of it go hand in hand. They have, on a larger scale, something of the character of the old lutenist-songs. The fingers of the lutenist were directly expressive, as are the keys of the piano. Two centuries of development had given men a greatly extended range of musical thought and suggestive association, and Schubert could arouse and apply these memories and these new idioms to the enhancement of a new poetic imagery. He could embrace in music the mental and emotional experiences of an expanding humanity.

The musical ascendancy of Germany in the nineteenth century began at home. Nowhere else in the world was the household cultivation of the art so widespread and so fine in its sensitiveness and taste. Sonatas, songs, trios, and quartets poured from the minds of her composers, and from the presses of her publishers, because thousands of accomplished families were ready to absorb them. Composers are not rare phenomena, nor is music an esoteric art. It lives by virtue of the people who practise it, and what they ask for will be supplied. Music too remotely beyond them, or too blatantly beneath their taste, will quickly die. It was the domestic standard of German music which could select and accept the songs of men like Brahms and Wolf. France and Italy were mainly busy with more public and spectacular forms. England had plenty of homely effort, but a very low standard of value. The songs of

Parry and Stanford were not unworthy to stand beside
those of Germany, but they had to fight a flood of sentimental mediocrity of well-nigh universal popularity.
We paid thus for our ignorance. Our most educated
classes had the crudest musical ideas. Our publicists,
our merchants, our scientists, and our men of letters
were, with few exceptions, confessed philistines. A
populace which, having just learnt to read, demanded
cheap fiction and sensational journalism, was matched
by an aristocracy which flaunted its artistic poverty of
ideas and practised a rank emotionalism. This treacly
tide has ebbed, but it takes time to build informed
opinion, and the task is all the harder when a nation's
social leaders have neither direct experience nor acquired knowledge of an art.

Educationally we are making decided progress, and
it is beginning in the right place, among the children
and in our schools. Beethoven wrote a few easy pieces
for his pupils. Schumann a great many. Schumann's
charming and fanciful titles too often accompanied a
musical idiom which was not so easy for the young
hand and mind to grasp. But since his time a great deal
of music has been written which is excellently designed
to foster a pleasant and graded education. All the folk-
songs and all the easier classics have been edited to this
end, and there are few musical homes which have not
resounded to the playing by children of these aids to
proficiency and taste. The school singing-class is
rapidly becoming, in its sphere, what the choir was to
the musical choir-boy. Italy made itself musical two or
three centuries ago by educating children. By far the
greater number of the most talented composers in every
country began life in a church choir. It will be interesting to see if modern schools can discover and foster

the latent abilities of present generations to a comparable extent.

Meanwhile, our homes are being invaded by the machines. It has often been remarked that there are whole categories of music which were evolved solely for the delight of the performer. The listener as such has no standing in them. The madrigal is a type of such music. It is not intended to appeal to the listener very directly, and it is in fact difficult for any one not a potential singer to appreciate what is happening in the interplay of parts. The subtleties of expression are all internal. This is to some extent true of the older chamber music too. It is the player who gets the full value of the thought, both in his own part and by immersion in those of his partners. But one might not unreasonably go further and say that there has never been any music at all which did not address itself primarily to the performer. This is certainly true up to quite modern times. Each single part had to make musical sense, and not merely add arbitrary notes to a general logic of effect. The craftsmanship of composition has therefore always involved a clear understanding of the 'feel' of an instrument and the 'lie' of a voice. Many failures have been due to the putting of musical matter in the wrong place, and it was normally taken as an axiom that a composer should know with practical certainty what were the peculiar virtues of his instruments.

And does not this also apply in its degree to the listener? Is it possible, for example, to distinguish between the types of melody suited to a voice or to a violin, respectively, without at least an inkling of their methods of production? The question is not academic, because a public verdict may well depend on the public understanding of these distinctions. People who have

no instinctive or informed views of the differing building qualities of wood, stone, and concrete can never
have a reliable judgement on architectural forms. The
differences between an organ and an orchestra are of
this same fundamental nature. Men who handle them
are expected to feel their qualities keenly. But even
those who merely listen to the finished product should
gather, at least imaginatively, a fair conception of the
proper use of the various types of musical means. There
has never been any substantial or permanent progress
without this enlightened appreciation on the part of
those whose support was vital.

An interesting example of the effect of this direct
knowledge is shown by that machine which first seriously challenged the competent performer. The player-
piano abolishes all the difficulties of hand-technique
as applied to the keyboard. It also abolishes most of the
expressive subtleties. The simpler models provided
levers and pedals by which the performer could control
the pace of the music, and to some extent the details of
emphasis and pedalling. But it was clear from the first
that a man who could play the piano in the normal way,
however clumsily, could do far more with the player-piano
than could those who knew nothing of the keyboard
directly. The pianist knew at least what he was trying
to obtain from the mechanism, and he sometimes got
convincing results. The non-player was greatly handicapped, and had to progress by what was in fact imaginative practice. The player-piano had great merits. It
opened the whole literature of the piano to those who
could not otherwise approach it directly, it could play
arrangements, it could repeat again and again, and it left
a fair margin of discretion to the operator. Later models
have gone further. They have offered a completely

mechanical production, notes, pace, interpretation and all. This abolishes the amateur performer completely, and raises a very important issue. If, hitherto, the whole character of the art of music has been intimately bound up with the direct personal practice of it, by experts and amateurs alike, what will happen if this active participation ceases? What kind of control or influence can be exercised by music-lovers as a whole, if their only direct connexion with the art is reduced to the pressing of an electric switch?

THE STAGE

THE STAGE

I

As soon as men are able to think at all, they begin to ponder on their surroundings. The most primitive pursuits of food and shelter involve questions about the nature of the world, the sun and seasons, wind and rain, and the behaviour of plants and animals. These common sights and sounds present a baffling mixture of processes. Some appear to be fairly regular in sequence, and thus encourage simple ideas of cause and effect. Some are unaccountably irregular and capricious. In the early stages of civilization the mental grasp of natural order is very narrow. There is a wide margin of events of which no convincing explanation can be given, and the very habit of seeking such an explanation is one of the latest, as it is also one of the surest, fruits of intellectual progress. To the savage, nature is herself a savage, wilful and jealous and interfering, and all the chances of life are put on the hither side of direct knowledge. They are held to be unnatural or supernatural, as the case may be. They must come from another world, a world of spirits or influences which are beyond exact foresight and control. And as soon as man can form a plausible theory of these wayward powers, he gives them names and attributes. They become the basis of his religion.

It is of the utmost importance to primitive beings that they should be able to stand in some kind of definite relation to these external arbiters of fate, so far as any theory of their behaviour can be surmised. There may be signs and portents to be discerned by careful observation. At the very least man may show that he is

constantly anxious and expectant. If there is anything
he can do to make clear even the smallest hint of a
supernatural order, he will do it. His fears are deep
and urgent. His awe and his wonder are grounded in
an overwhelming sense of helplessness. If by the expression of ardour and anxiety, by any act of homage or
contrition, he can arouse the attention of a controlling
and superhuman spirit, he will by so much be nearer to
the possible fulfilment of his desires. He cannot bear
either the dark silence or the dim uncertainties of the
gods. If they will not speak, then he must. He must
make plain by word and gesture the nature of the
secrets he would have revealed. That is the beginning
of religious ritual. If his speech becomes still plainer,
if he goes so far as to represent by some form of action
the events he seeks to control or understand, that is
the beginning of drama. It matters little whether the
counterfeit is natural, as in the rites of war or hunting
or husbandry, or whether it inclines to magic, as in the
search for spells and potions; so far as words and
gestures try by representation to make plain the fears
and desires of men, the result is drama, and drama of
the most moving and elemental kind.

This intimate relation between religion, ritual, and
drama is one of the axioms of scholarship. The origins
of drama are to be found in the mists of ancient ritual.
Ritual is the expression of religious thought and emotion, the attempt to approach and realize the ultimate
nature of the unseen world. It is no accident that, from
the 'Prometheus' of Aeschylus to the 'Parsifal' of
Wagner, the greatest poets of the stage have used it to
portray the last transcendencies of religious and philosophic thought. Shakespeare tells us 'all the world's
a stage'. The stage, for its part, has constantly

endeavoured to be a microcosm of the whole world, known and unknown, real and imaginary, material and spiritual, seen and unseen. And this is why the stage has so often shown alternate periods of reform and decay ɪ ɔt uni ᴋe the changing elements of religious and ritualis ic history. An accepted symbolism becomes a convention, a convention decays into a lifeless formula, the stage sinks to the level of an entertainment, to the devices of an ephemeral spectacle. Then comes a poet-evangelist, fired by the magnificence of an old tradition or by the vision of a new faith, and he sees in the theatre an allegory of the whole web of life, an ideal place for the vivid presentment not only of human character and fortune, but of superhuman powers and destinies. The stage becomes in his hands a temple worthy of the sublimest flights of intuition, thought, and imagery. In all discussions of drama, of its action, its poetry, its setting, and its music, we have constantly to remember not only what it is at any particular period of its history, but what it has been in the gradual unfolding of human beliefs, and what it yet might be in their further evolution. Nowhere in the arts can the limitations of reality so nearly reach the ideal. Nowhere can a vision of resplendent truth be so easily clouded or destroyed.

In the history of drama, and particularly with reference to dramatic music, the Western Church played a notable part. It furnishes at least one striking example of a dramatic ritual which became at length an independent artistic form of the highest order. It was the custom in the Church of the earliest Middle Ages to recite in Holy Week the story of the Passion, and to recite it in music. This tradition may even go back in essence to the fourth or fifth centuries of our era. The Latin of the chosen Evangelist was sung to plain-chant.

H

The narrator was one of the Deacons of the Passion. It further seemed appropriate that the words of Jesus should be sung by another voice, so as to mark their special origin and significance. From this it was a small step to introduce a third Deacon, who sang the words of Pilate, of Peter, of the disciples, soldiers, and Jews. These three Deacons of the Passion, traditionally Tenor, Bass, and Alto, thus gave a dramatic representation of the gospel narrative to the extent of clearly separating the chief figures in it. In this medieval ritual begins the wonderful evolution of Passion Music, and indirectly of Oratorio in some of its main features. The division of voices, for example, and the type of voice traditionally used, have never been completely forgotten. The Jesus of Bach is a Bass, his Evangelist is a Tenor. There was probably a thousand years of custom behind this choice.

The use of a chorus to mark the shouts of the people, or to sing any words recorded as being spoken by many voices, was a clear line of advance. There were more contemplative settings of the Passion story which used a chorus throughout. The Reformation brought the translated texts, and Germany in particular found an overflowing well of inspiration in the dramatic vigour of its own speech. Against the narration of the Evangelist were contrasted the interpolated words of the chief figures in the Passion story, together with those of a chorus of disciples or Jews. Add a contemplative chorus to express the emotions of the faithful to whom the drama is being unfolded, and we have the whole form as it was used with such skill and beauty by Heinrich Schütz in the seventeenth century. Plainsong had become on the one hand recitative, or musical narration, and on the other hand versified melody, fitted to congregational hymns. Passion music then expands into the Church Cantata, which can take for its theme any incident or passage in Scripture. Innumerable settings of the Passion story were written by German church musicians, following those of the older church in Italy. The tradition culminates in Bach.

The dramatic instinct of the Church was by no means confined to this central theme. There are recorded directions to the priests officiating on Easterday that they might well suggest, by ritual movement and gesture, the search of the empty tomb and the discovery of the Resurrection. There were mystery plays of all kinds, some of very crude type, some containing the germs of later and finer ideals. Incidents in the lives of the saints and patriarchs were acted, with homely and realistic settings. What could be more natural than a real cradle and manger for the Nativity? The figures were themselves so familiar that it was easy to make the story vivid. And if there were shepherds, why not also the shepherd's pipe? And when the shepherds told of the heavenly host, could not the choir sing 'Gloria in excelsis'? Music itself might thus at times be part of the story. The records of these sacred plays of the Middle Ages are usually connected with the choir. The choristers of St. Paul's in London were taught to perform mystery and morality plays as late as the fourteenth century.

The morality play was for edification. It personified good and evil, wisdom and folly, truth and falsehood. It set out to present an allegory of the temptations and opportunities which might occur to every man. It was also, like the parable, a means of teaching an unlettered audience a great many of the past events and present problems of society. It presented dramatically that general view of the world which the preaching friars taught by homely illustration and eloquence. Our reforming Bishop Latimer, as late as the sixteenth century, could preach a long Sermon on the Plough, even a Sermon on the Cards. Every feature of ordinary life could be made into a text, and the more familiar the theme the easier it was to point a moral. Thus morality plays were by no means confined to subjects of solemn discussion. There was even a large element of comedy in many of them, and a frequent descent, not unnatural in rough and rustic actors, into active buffoonery. The comic could not be kept out of the picture, for real life is frequently ridiculous, and the wit of the Middle Ages was thoroughly objective. Puritans might condemn, but no expounding of the more sober virtues could abolish all the fun of the fair. The fabric of drama, like the web of life itself, is sometimes a tragedy and sometimes a joke. The Middle Ages accepted both with gusto.

From the church to the churchyard, thence to the village green or rough booth of a fair, these are the steps from sacred to secular drama, but all the main elements, from the highest ideals to the broadest farce, were present in the one as in the other. There was always a lively difference of opinion about the whole custom. Some would have abolished it altogether, and the Church itself sometimes took this view. Others preached reform, and tried to keep clear in mind the potential virtues and ideals of the stage. The controversy went on for centuries. It still exists, wherever the subject is seriously discussed. So far as the true mystery or sacred drama is concerned, the Church did in fact decree its abolition, with one or two exceptions. There is a survival at Ober-Ammergau, which was

specially licensed on conditions of drastic and permanent reform. Ober-Ammergau has retained both
the direct dramatic methods of the Middle Ages and
the simple dignity of presentation which later reforms
have brought. It is perhaps our most interesting link
with those far-off times when religious drama was at
once a ritual of the Church and an art of the people.

2

The year 1600 is usually held to fix the first achievements of Opera and Oratorio in Italy, but like most of
the dates in artistic progress it is a convenient reminder
rather than strict truth. New forms do not appear thus
suddenly, for the imagination of the artist can only
work freely when it has at least a fair background of
accepted idioms to stimulate it. The most original
genius is mainly concerned in setting old ideals in a new
light. Opera and Oratorio were not suddenly invented.
They both grew out of a professed desire to revive the
past, and there were few of their distinguishing features
which were not frankly founded on what their authors
believed to be proved and classical traditions. There
had always been a certain relation between drama and
music. What marked the innovators of Italy was a
determination to seek guidance from sources still older
than those of which the centuries immediately preceding
them had knowledge. Their ideals were Greek, and
belong to the general revival of Greek literature and
drama which was one of the most important consequences of the Renaissance of the arts.

Towards the end of the sixteenth century a group of
Italian musicians and men of letters were studying
Greek drama. They were impressed by the very inti-
mate connexion which appeared to exist between words

and music as the Greeks had used them. Not only did
the Greek Chorus chant its verses, but there was
evidence that the whole drama had been conceived in
tones as well as in words. Vocal inflexions and cadences
were inseparably connected with the Greek art of the
stage, and this song-speech seemed to these Italian
students to be the essential foundation of all truly
dramatic music. They wished to keep the dramatic
action as natural and as flexible as possible, but they
also desired to enhance the emotional value of the words
by clothing them in music. Neither the polyphonic
part-writing of the madrigal nor the versified tunes of
lyric songs could do this. There must be a 'new music',
highly malleable in itself and yet rigidly subservient to
the words. This, so it seemed, was the problem which
Greece had solved. Why should it not be adapted, with
equal success, to more modern musical idioms?

The music of the Greek stage is a subject of which we
know in detail very little, and the sixteenth century
probably knew less. Our ideas of Greek melody are
still mainly theoretical. But it is at least clear that the
Greeks set the very highest store by the combined arts
of music and dramatic poetry, and it is also clear that
they achieved this union without spoiling the action of
the drama. The story is unfolded without interruption,
and with sustained eloquence. Music is used to em-
phasize the purport of the words, but it does not clog
the march of events. These are the fundamental
assumptions of music-drama. The details of the Greek
method is conjectural. The details of our own more
modern attempts to combine music and drama have
been the occasions of controversy more heated and
more bitter than any other musical problem in our
history. The quarrel is indeed still rife. It seems to be

inherent in the form, and we may never find an agreed solution.

To begin with, we have a vastly more complicated apparatus of expression than ever the Greeks can have imagined. It is possible, in theory, for words to be sung at a pace and with an intonation not too far removed from those of speech, and remain to this extent natural and free in utterance. This is the ideal, a genuine speech-rhythm. But what can an orchestra do with the indeterminate accents and phrases of speech? All ensemble playing needs the discipline of measured time and unanimous standards of phrasing. When the singer is added, he also must obey these or similar musical conventions. He cannot sing as he would speak. His words must be made to fit the prevailing pattern of the concerted sound. He becomes in fact a highly conventionalized figure, which only a lively imagination can accept as a satisfactory symbol of the reality he is intended to interpret. If the convention is carried far enough he becomes a puppet, an animated musical instrument, so far removed from normal human behaviour that he is incredible in any situation involving ordinary standards of reality. This drift towards a purely artificial and symbolic method of representation has occurred time after time in the history of dramatic music. It happens too in drama without music.

No man ever spoke in real life as Hamlet speaks. Poetic drama is just as much a convention as is music-drama. Speech and behaviour alike have to give way to the inspiration of the poet, who does what he pleases with words and actions on the stage, in order that his poetic diction and symbolism may have free play. When, as often happens, such a drama is written by a man lacking in poetic gifts, the result is pure formalism, too clearly unreal to be tolerable. Shakespeare's dramas without Shakespeare's poetry would be grotesque. The conventions of music-drama are grotesque for exactly the same reasons. Only a white heat of imagination can sustain the accumulated unrealities of the poetic or musical stage. When Keats wrote 'Beauty is truth, truth beauty' he spoke as a poet, not as a dramatist. All truths are not beautiful, nor is the beautiful literally true. And just as we differ in our individual judgements of poetic beauty, so we differ in our conceptions of poetic truth. To those whose sense of poetry is rudimentary, poetic drama is a caricature. To those whose musical experience is narrow, music-drama is a flat and tiresome convention.

And the problem is still further complicated by the fact that it cuts across just those musical intuitions which we feel most keenly and therefore watch most jealously. Those who prefer musical beauty to dramatic truth, to whom music is music first and foremost, will resent anything which sacrifices this purer art to a preoccupation with external ideas and actions, however important. Those whose dramatic instinct is stronger than their purely musical sensitiveness will permit all kinds of violations of musical canons for the sake of a more convincing dramatic reality. Every dramatic reform of opera has had to face the vehement opposition of a large proportion of contemporary musicians. Every reformer has had to ignore or condemn the musical instincts of his fellow artists and appeal to the dramatic response of a wider and less specialized public. The early Italian reformers did this no less than the Gluckists and Wagnerians of later times. They proclaimed a 'new music', consciously narrative and representational in style, and deliberately sacrificing the coherence and beauty of the older music in pursuit of what they held to be the superior claims of dramatic truth.

Their solution of the verbal problem, of the difficulty of giving words something of the pace and clarity of speech, was the extensive use of recitative. By meticulous attention to accents and inflexions it is possible to put into musical notation a passable equivalent for the pitch and speed of formal elocution. This is recitative in its simplest and most consistent form. It is already a long way from natural speech, because a singer must be given definite notes, and these are few, while the intonations of speech are infinite. And this is where music begins to creep in. The moment a composer allows himself to include a purely musical thought in the vocal line, he so far leaves the rigid translation of words into notes. He becomes by so much a musician rather than a dramatist, and the more musical he is the more difficult will he find it to resist the constant temptation to hold up both the words and actions of his singers in order to express his more exclusively musical ideas. This inherent conflict of aims is clearly evident even in the most thorough-going recitative of the earliest examples. The pure art of melody suddenly usurps the chief place, in an emotional pause or in the turn of a phrase, and for that moment composer and singer together have left the real and entered the poetic world. Truth has had to leave room for beauty. The handling of words and music together is a compromise, none the less delicate even when genius appears to find a perfect balance intuitively.

The Italian reformers had Greece in mind, and their recitative is of the simplest possible structure. The accompaniment is no more than a few chords used mainly as marks of punctuation. The problem of using

a whole orchestra of players at the same time does not
arise. Even so, these men could not withstand the
temptation to put in snatches of melody, often very
beautiful in themselves, but not strict recitative. And
when this new music got into the hands of a specifically
musical genius, nothing could prevent him from in-
corporating, by one device or another, all the various
kinds of pure music, old or new, which his imagination
could create. The singers were equally inconsistent.
They were ready to act, but they wanted to sing as well.
Interminable recitative is no substitute for vocal
melody. More potent than all was the emphatic voice
of the public. People who preferred pure drama
could go to the playhouse. Those who came to the
Opera came for music, amongst other things, and strict
recitative is sheer weariness to men whose notions of
music are melody, and harmony, and the infinite
suggestiveness of tone-colours and interweaving parts.

It is constantly asserted that the opponents of operatic reform were stupidly blind to the essential ideals of
musical drama. It would be far truer to say that they
were too strictly musical to tolerate the inconsistencies
of an art so inherently illogical. It was music they were
fighting for, and if the drama interfered, as they felt it,
with the music, then they condemned without scruple.
They may have failed to realize that the dramatic
instinct is itself one of the most powerful incentives to
purely musical inspiration, but the future has justified
them at least this far, that no reform of opera has ever
succeeded by virtue of a dramatic theory, however
convincing. Every successful innovator has had to
prove himself a great musician, in the absolute sense
of the term, theory or no theory. He has had to
offer a music which was convincing in itself, whatever

sense of the dramatic may have underlain his achievement.

Two works were produced in the year 1600 which embodied the new dramatic point of view. One was an oratorio, Cavalieri's 'La Rappresentazione di Anima e di Corpo', the other an opera, Peri's 'Euridice'. The oratorio was performed in the Oratory of St. Philip Neri's church in Rome. St. Philip had in the previous century founded the congregation of the Oratorians. He had been a keen patron of sacred music, and his sermons were frequently followed by dramatic and musical versions of a sacred story, appropriate discourses being given between the acts. A stage setting with costumes was used, and there was at first no distinction in method between these sacred oratorios (the name comes from the Oratory) and the secular opera of the theatre. Cavalieri's 'Soul and Body' is a mystery play in the medieval tradition. The characters are Time, Life, the World, Pleasure, Intellect, the Soul, and the Body. There was a prologue, choruses, and dances. A small orchestra accompanied and played short interludes (*ritornelli*). The Overture was a madrigal with instrumental accompaniment. The players of instruments were to be hidden, and there were precise directions regarding the dresses and scenery. The story is an allegory of the vanity of earthly riches. Cavalieri uses recitative for purposes of musical narration, and his work draws together, as it were, all the various stage methods which his own and previous centuries had found serviceable.

For a short time oratorio and opera followed the same dramatic lines, the one sacred or mystical, the other secular. But by the middle of the seventeenth century oratorio had in the main left the stage, and become more akin to Passion music. Carissimi, a very gifted Italian composer, one of whose works, 'Jephtha', is still a moving example of musical and dramatic sensitiveness, follows the method of Passion music in using a Narrator to sing in recitative such parts of the story as might in earlier days have been acted on the stage. His work therefore gives us the form of oratorio in its modern guise. It becomes a sacred concert, using a dramatic musical technique, but dispensing with scenery and action. Its place hereafter is in the concert-hall, whether this be a church used for that purpose, or a theatre where for the time being the normal apparatus of the stage is allowed to remain idle.

The features of opera proper, as the Italian reformers understood them, can be studied at their best in the works of Monteverde, whose 'Orpheus' was produced in 1607. It is significant that the story is Greek, and it is a story almost uniquely suited for dramatic music, because the mainspring of the action is inherently musical. It is a Greek myth concerning the power of music, and the number of settings of it written by the early composers of opera reminds us of the way in which the Greek dramatists themselves used certain familiar and mythical themes again and again in their classical dramas. There is a Greek atmosphere in the treatment too. The action, though dramatic in emotion, is often indirect and statuesque. There is a great deal of narration. There is direct intervention of super-natural powers, a device also characteristic of Greek sources. The chorus comments on the story, like the Greek chorus. The orchestra—the very word is Greek —is used with clear understanding of the contrasted associations of various instruments. Just as the Greeks felt one melodic mode to differ profoundly in mood from another, one being martial, one plaintive, a third enervating in atmosphere, so Monteverde used the instruments of his orchestra not so much to build up a complicated fabric of sound as to give to the various dramatic situations what he felt to be their appropriate instrumental colours. He thus initiated a practice which has been a steadily increasing feature in the evolution of stage music, changes of mood being often more vividly illustrated by the quality of the instrumental accompaniment than by the vocal parts sung by the actual actors in the drama. Monteverde's orchestra included viols and violins, harp, guitars, harpsichords, organs (no doubt small and portable), trombones, trumpets, and cornets. These gave him a wide range of instrumental colour, and he used them, as they were suitable, for special effects. The accompaniment of a solo voice was in the main a simple harmonic background which punctuated the recitative, but there are *ritornelli* and short symphonies where groups of instruments are employed with a clear consciousness of their emotional colour. The overture, which is frankly a preliminary fanfare, serves to arrest the attention of the audience. There are massive choruses and elaborate dances. The ritual of the dance is as ancient and venerable as drama itself, and it has always appealed with especial force to those societies whose sense of the stage was keen.

Monteverde was master of all the known forms of music of his day. He could write the old polyphony and the old dances, the new recitative and the new melody, he was acutely sensitive to the enlarging vocabulary of harmony, and thoroughly alive to the varied associations of his instruments. All these accomplishments, combined with a dramatic instinct amounting to genius, made him incomparably the best exponent

of the new movement. Had it been possible to
ensure a succession of equally able men and, what is
rarer still, a public that could assess dramatic sincerity
at its proper value, the subsequent story of opera would
have been less chequered. It might have been possible
steadily to pursue those dramatic and musical ideals
which have in fact inspired every reformer, but which
have been as constantly engulfed by the more superficial tastes of smaller men, and by the unthinking
verdicts of an insensitive public.

3

The diseases of the stage are public diseases. That is
the crucial fact in the fortunes of Italian opera. Opera
is music definitely addressed to a general public. It is
intended to convince a comparatively untutored audience that music can illustrate and help the emotional
purport of a dramatic situation. A dozen other appeals are being made to the same bar of opinion at the
same time. There are dances, dresses, scenery, and
mechanical transformations of ever-increasing ingenuity. There is the story itself and such remnants of prose
or verse as may be clearly audible. There is the art of
the actor, including all the devices of expression and
gesture which are calculated to awaken a direct and
magnetic response. All these varied elements are displayed under the utmost possible glamour of limelight,
and in a building purposely designed to encourage an
atmosphere of social enjoyment and success. The
apostles of the new dramatic music, whether they
realized it or not, were in fact appealing to a new public.
That public had incalculable tastes, and the future was
in its hands. The first public opera-house was built in
Venice in 1637. The audience did not altogether pay

the piper. Opera is far too expensive a spectacle to survive by public support alone. There has always been private munificence behind it. But it is inherently a public art, and though the public only partially pays, it certainly calls the tune.

This is the momentous change which distinguishes the seventeenth century. Gone is the old cloistered ideal, which held music to be a vocation not unfit to rank with other sacred arts and rites. The intimacies of chamber-music are taking new and beautiful forms, but their quality is essentially select and private. Musical progress, in the general estimation, has stepped literally into the limelight. To be a fine singer is to be an operatic singer. To be a famous composer is to be the writer of successful operas. The new art of music has thus taken to fancy dress, accepted every species of theatrical ornament, and asked for the applause of the market-place.

And what a public it was! Those private little boxes recall Ruskin's remark about gardens with iron railings: 'Thieves outside or lunatics inside'. The theatre box is a survival of caste, of highs and lows, nobles and shop-keepers, touchables and untouchables. It was convenient for receiving friends or for avoiding acquaintances. A few congenial guests could chatter and eat and drink and play cards together. And chatter, eat, drink, and play they did. When we read of the spectacular triumphs of a handful of famous names, we are rarely conscious of the thousands of aspiring singers who were never given a tolerable hearing at all. The manners of the public opera-house were at best those of a fashionable assembly-room, at worst those of a bear-garden. There is indeed more than a hint of the old bear-baiting amphitheatre in the shape and proportions of a conven-

tional theatre. The boxes of an opera-house should be
seen from the stage. They look like a fantastic zoo.
These cubicles with a missing wall still flaunt much
vulgar ostentation, much social punctilio, much fashionable affectation. Imagine them filled with people who
behaved exactly as if they were receiving friends at
home. Fashionable operatic audiences used to pay
hardly more attention to the stage than is now paid to
the horses at a race-meeting. They looked for the
favourite and applauded. They listened for a few
minutes and then returned to gossip and cards. The
manners of the pit were no better, but certainly no
worse. There are stories of quite famous virtuosi being
literally inaudible, their music completely engulfed in
the general hubbub. This was the new temple of music,
the place for which thousands of operas were written,
thousands of players and singers recruited and trained.
Small wonder that the music itself soon began to show
something other than the ideals of Greek drama.

On the stage the individual singer inevitably became
the most important factor. If the singers could not
please the audience, then the opera was a failure,
whatever its own intrinsic merits. The pleasure of
average ears is in simple melodies and infectious
rhythms. Restrained and careful characterization is a
mere waste of time if the audience will not trouble to
listen. Nor could the singers themselves afford to be
ignored. They had to stake everything on the chance
of capturing the public ear, and to effect this they
needed, not recitatives, but songs. They could dress up
and posture and act, but their chief gift was a trained
voice, and whatever their dramatic function they must
have music which would display their voices. In a very
short time the main ingredient of Italian opera was not

classical drama, but effective singing, not dry narration, but easy melody and clever ornamentation. A string of suitable airs was held together by patches of conventional recitative. It was the airs that every one wanted to hear, and the drama was tolerated only so far as it gave them a setting.

It is surprising that the actual quality of the music remained as good as it did. There were many passages both of real dramatic power and of lyric inspiration within these illogical chains of formal tunes. There was fine workmanship that had not the slightest chance of being properly heard. Composers, players, and singers were constantly improving their technique and offering a steadily widening range of control and accomplishment. From time to time a patron, or a group of enthusiasts, would support productions of exceptional and sterling merit. They could not ignore the public, but they could to some extent choose what should be put before it. Patrons were of course dangerously susceptible to intrigue, and to the personal blandishments of performers, but they had at least a wish to discriminate and some power of effective choice.

The effects of the patronage system are clearly seen under Louis XIV in France. There Lulli, Italian-born and a keen student of other men's work, combined the qualities of an astute and unscrupulous courtier with those of a talented composer and producer. He was an able administrator as well. His operas strike a mean between the original claims of drama and the public preference for attractive music. His subjects are mainly classical. Through all its varied musical fashions, serious opera retained a decided bias towards the Greek stories and myths which were its first themes. In the court of Louis such stories were the safest, from every

I

point of view. The King and his favourites would
not tolerate anything which savoured of critical comment on public events. Even a distant parallel had to
be very carefully disguised, or the writer might find
himself an exile. It was better on every ground to
picture a conveniently unreal world. Greek myths also
had the merit of including supernatural beings and
miraculous interventions. These gave opportunities to
the stage mechanics, who could count on warm applause
if they could devise new and striking scenic effects.
Room had also to be found for elaborate dances, with
a good show of pretty faces and becoming costumes.
The beauty-chorus is not a modern invention. There
were singers who had to be kept in good humour by
songs which suited them, and by which they in turn
could delight the king and his friends. There was the
orchestra, and here Lulli was a real innovator. His
overtures, which consisted of a slow and arresting
introduction followed by a lively fugue, were exactly
suited to the conditions of performance in the theatre.
They began by awaking the attention of the listener,
and proceeded to put him into a cheerful and appreciative mood. So successful was this type of overture
that it became an accepted form of orchestral music,
suitable for all public occasions. It had nothing to do
with the drama which followed, and could be used for
any setting. Handel's overture to 'The Messiah' is a
typical example of the form. All these varied elements
of the stage Lulli mastered and controlled, and contrived at the same time to keep the special favour of
Louis. He supplanted every rival, became an ennobled
and naturalized Frenchman, acquired a monopoly of
opera and Court music, and amassed a fortune.

There is a popular impression that musicians are

unpractical dreamers. They are supposed to live in a world where the ordinary standards of social and commercial competence are unknown. Like the artist of romantic fiction, they are held to be the absolute negation of business ability. Nothing could well be farther from the truth, in the sphere of stage musicianship at least. A busy writer and producer of operas performs a task beside which most of the problems of commerce and administration are child's-play. Every possible difficulty, alike personal, material, and financial, is his daily lot. He has to organize and focus a combination of efforts which touch every conceivable side of artistic life. He has to co-ordinate all these activities at a precise place and at a precise moment. One weak link in the chain may destroy him. Months of hard and thankless labour may result in an hour's glory or a year's ruin. This is one of the fascinations of the stage. It is the supreme artistic gamble. Patrons, composers, and performers alike feel that of all artistic ventures opera is both the most exciting and the most exacting. It is also the most comprehensive. Poets, painters, and musicians, architects and engineers, dancers and masters of ceremony, carpenters and mechanics, all have a hand in it. It includes every known form of musical material. An opera-house is a small kingdom, comprising and controlling many artistic provinces, and there have been few men who, given the chance, have not coveted its resources. It exists by favour of those who are ready to stake their wealth and reputation on it. It is emphatically not the place for the unpractical idealist.

The prestige of Louis and Lulli was immense. More than an echo of it came to England. Charles II in exile had seen Louis take a stately part in Lulli's ballets. He had seen the magnificence of the French court and the genuine artistic quality of many of its tastes. He was not of a temperament to dwell too deeply on the ultimate value of social arts, but he found in England a society tired of puritanical repressions, and perhaps on this account the more ready to think its own type of masque and pageantry parochial and old-fashioned. Charles brought a touch of artistic cosmopolitanism which easily captured the ear of his aristocratic friends. He wished to import to London something of the artistic fashions and repute of France. It was the beginning, as it was perhaps also the end, of English opera. Purcell wrote one coherent masterpiece, 'Dido and Aeneas', but he wrote it for a girl's school, not for the Restoration theatre. This work remains a somewhat wistful monument of a past which had no future. It is in every respect superior to any dramatic music then existing, either at home or abroad. It is more original, more beautiful, and more dramatically consistent than Lulli at his best. There is no contemporary Italian work equal to it. If ever we evolve an opera we can really call our own, 'Dido and Aeneas' will be its most cherished legacy.

The works which Purcell wrote for the public stage were operas only by some stretching of the term. The public wanted engaging songs and lively dances, and Purcell could provide these with unfailing freshness and beauty. It also wanted exotic scenery, strange costumes, and new mechanical ingenuities. And no one could hit off an odd situation in music better than Purcell could. Of consistent plot, reasoned character-drawing, or indeed any of the dramatic conditions of credibility, there was no need, for these things were not in demand. What was desired was a variety entertainment, and the disjointed operas of Purcell supplied it. There are

isolated scenes of great musical beauty, with many
a moment of inspired resource. There are delightful
songs and duets, grave and gay, on which Purcell
lavished his incomparable gifts of melody and word-
painting, and there are scores of preludes, interludes,
and dances which are perennially fragrant. These gems
remain, but they are immersed in a mass of inconse-
quent and incongruous incidents, and they have never
recovered from this initial chaos. Purcell's public had
no wish for the consistent unfolding of an extended and
unified design. They wanted a dramatic and musical
medley. They got what they wanted, and the first and
most golden chance of a native opera vanished in the
process. If Purcell had had the opportunities of some
of his contemporaries in Italy and France, every opera-
house in Europe would have clamoured for his music.
He might in due time have been imported back into
England, and given the status rarely bestowed on an
Englishman-born.

In Italy the triumphs of the singers reached resounding dimensions. Italian opera became the school of all
artists of the first quality, and a reputation won in
Italy carried its possessor into every fashionable
theatre in Europe. The Italian method of education
was very effective, though it was in some respects
more drastic and unscrupulous than would have been
tolerated in other times and places. The idea of a
musical conservatorium, like the word which describes
it, comes from the Italy of the seventeenth and eighteenth centuries. These schools were in origin usually
charitable foundations for the education of poor
children. The music they fostered must have greatly
varied in quality, but they captured a promising voice
young, and in view of the insatiable public demand for

powerful and trained voices, there was every induce-
ment to exploit any vocal gift to the full. Italy then
produced a steady supply of composers, singers, and
players more highly trained than any to be found elsewhere. The stage employed them and was itself a hard
and unflinching taskmaster. The repute of Italian
singers and teachers has survived to our own day.

Further, there was a very strong temptation to
preserve a voice at almost any cost. One notorious
custom, frequently practised, cannot be ignored in any
balanced description of the musical tastes and circumstances of the time. The unnatural preservation of
boys' voices became a custom frequently and tacitly
accepted. There is no doubt that the vast majority of
these unnatural sopranos were produced by methods
commonly used in the Moslem courts of the Near East.
The convenient fiction of a disabling accident was
sometimes used to calm an awakening public con-
science, but the facts were perfectly well known, and
a young chorister's potential prospects were carefully
weighed. Legal and ecclesiastical vetoes were equally
powerless against the glittering prizes which an exceptional voice could win. Male sopranos, having the
pitch of a boy's voice with the power of a man's lungs,
sang the upper parts in some of the most famous choirs
of the Italian Church. They found themselves in great
demand for the newer arts of the stage. Their vocal
range was not so great as that of a woman, but their
voices were exceptionally strong, they had spent a life-
time in the acquisition of perfect control and flexibility,
and it hardly seems to have occurred to the applauding
public as a whole that there was anything wrong·in this
extreme exploitation of a physical disability.

The whole cult was in keeping with many of the most

popular, and to our later eyes the most revolting,
spectacles which attracted the European public of
those times. The parade of captured savages, of physical
monstrosities, of exotic animals, often under conditions
of extreme cruelty and degradation, were common
sights throughout Europe. Bear-baiting, cock-fighting,
and the grosser forms of athletic exercise did not offend
public opinion so much as do their mildest survivals in
our circuses and menageries to-day. From the gladia-
torial days of Rome down to the bull-fighting of
modern times there has always been an unthinking
public which judged an entertainment solely by its
power to excite and interest the spectator, not by its
cost to the unfortunate victim. On this plane the male
soprano was easily accepted, and he was in fact not so
much an unwilling victim as a pampered idol. He
suffered neither in repute nor reward. He was often
a man of intellectual as well as of musical distinction.
He sometimes became, like certain similar victims in
the East, an influential public counsellor and administrator.

Nothing is more characteristic of Italian opera, at
the height of its prestige, than this apotheosis of the
male soprano. Hundreds of operas were specifically
designed for him. He, the 'first man', was for a long
time far more important than the prima donna, or
'first woman'. It mattered not that the subject might be
a classical myth, the hero a Greek god. Hercules, on
the Italian operatic stage, was a male soprano, appro-
priately decked, crowing in his overpowering falsetto
elaborate versified travesties of what had been, in origin,
a godlike emotion. Nothing could show more clearly
the impossible gulf which has so frequently separated
dramatic ideals from operatic fashions. It became an

accepted convention that of the six personages then allowed for in the conventional operatic libretto, three should be women and three men. Of the three men two were usually sopranos, the third normally a tenor, though sometimes an alto. Rarely was there a bass, and only then as fourth man.

And these prime favourites of the public had to have their effective music, at whatever cost to the probabilities of character or story. There had to be emotional songs, dramatic songs, and songs with vocal gymnastics, all provided in an accepted sequence, in every act, and for every principal personage in turn. The only customary combination of voices was a duet between the *primo uomo* and the *prima donna*. This Grand Duo was essential, however artificially introduced. For the rest, no one singer could have two songs in succession, nor could two consecutive songs be of the same type. The finale had to employ the chorus and the ballet, this being as a rule the only appearance of the chorus in a musical function. Such were some of the artifices which the inordinate demand for exceptional singers engrafted on this far-famed opera of Italy, the envy and admiration of all who aspired to be connoisseurs and patrons of the stage.

The most remarkable fact of all, viewed from our later angle, is that in spite of these inane conventions, these emasculated singers, and the blatant and ill-mannered patronage which was too often their main support, there yet survived not only a great deal of musical competence, but many a permanent example of dramatic inspiration. Alessandro Scarlatti, for example, the father of Domenico, worked for this fickle public and under these artificial restraints. He wrote one hundred and fifteen operas, a fair index of the demand

for such works, and many of his contemporaries were
equally prolific. His plots and his chess-board of
characters follow the accepted models. His strings of
songs are threaded on the connecting recitative which
was all the dramatic verisimilitude his public would
accept. He had great gifts and did many things
supremely well. His handling of the orchestra helped
markedly to consolidate its organization along lines
which, so far as the strings were concerned, remained
permanent. He wrote excellent interludes and incidental music. His spontaneous command of lovely
Italian melody has given us many songs well worth
rescue from the stifling conventions which swallowed
the talent of lesser men. He did not often descend to
the perfunctory accompaniments which were all that
his public asked for or understood. By his genius he
contrived to bestow distinction on theatrical artifices
altogether unworthy of his talent. When we extract the
arias of Scarlatti, and those of his ablest contemporaries, for use in our concerts, we are paying a just
tribute to outstanding musical gifts. In consigning to
oblivion the many hundreds of Italian operas of that
period we may lose some such gems, but we are rightly
burying many distasteful evidences of social and artistic
abuses now happily forgotten.

4

In 1711 Handel captured London with an Italian opera,
'Rinaldo'. He wrote it in fourteen days and it was
lavishly staged. There was even a garden with a flight of
living birds. Not that this type of realistic effect was
unusual. Freschi's 'Berenice', produced at Padua in
1680, offered on the stage two lions, two elephants,
more than a hundred horses, and a forest scene with

wild boar, deer, and bears. Handel had travelled in
Italy and mastered the whole menagerie of operatic
devices. He came to London at a time when our aristocratic world was eager to taste these renowned and
exotic delights. 'Rinaldo' was a great success and inaugurated that long series of Italian operas by which
Handel sought to hold his public and make his own
fame and fortune. Fame he achieved, but fortune was
not so kind. Success brought rivalry, and an opposing
clique encouraged Buononcini, a contemporary composer of some repute, to challenge Handel's productions with another and equally sumptuous outfit.
Europe was scoured for the most famous singers, including of course the most famous male sopranos, by
the two rival parties. It is a sorry story, and its main
features have since been repeated times without number
both in England and America. The musicians did their
best, though the fact that Buononcini was held to be
a serious competitor with Handel shows what public
opinion, on the musical side of the question, was really
worth. The stage devoured money, the singers took
their fantastic fees, and the promoters became bankrupt.
As for the pursuit of high dramatic ideals, that was
entirely out of range.

Of opera in any sense native and human and natural,
there was not a trace. The only real gain in the whole
venture was the end of it. Handel finally gave up the
struggle and turned from opera in Italian to oratorio
in English. The views of some of the other participants
may be summed up in two sentences. A very renowned
importation of Handel's rivals, the male soprano
Farinelli, made a handsome fortune in three years,
returned to Italy, and built a fine villa. He called it
'The English Folly'. What many of the ordinary

spectators thought was neatly expressed in Byrom's epigram:

> Some say, compared to Bononcini,
> That Mynheer Handel's but a Ninny;
> Others aver, that he to Handel
> Is scarcely fit to hold a candle:
> Strange all this Difference should be,
> 'Twixt Tweedle-dum and Tweedle-dee.

Italian opera did not die, even in London. Thomas Arne had some success, though he was far less gifted than Handel, and the delightful songs for which he is remembered were written for less ambitious occasions. In opera Arne, like every other composer who wished to satisfy the fashionable taste of the time, had to shed every vestige of his genuinely native gifts and write the most convincing imitation of the Italian style which he could devise. Italian prestige was so overwhelming that for most societies which claimed to be cultured there was scarcely any other music worth serious attention. English, French, and German composers, whatever their natural talents, had to learn the Italian manner, use the Italian language, employ Italian singers, and count it a supreme success if their works were held fit to rank with the products of Naples or Rome. 'An exotic and irrational entertainment' was Dr. Johnson's verdict.

In Germany and Austria this obsession was often carried to absurd lengths. German-born singers, not proficient in Italian, sang in German, while at the same time and in the same opera imported Italians sang their parts in Italian. This odd strife of tongues has since happened nearer home, with mild apologies but with no loss of patronage, provided the foreign visitor was sufficiently famous. The practice, like so many other features of what at various times has passed for dramatic art, is simply one more proof of the fact that a casual public is utterly unfitted to recognize or encourage any but the most superficial artistic ideals. If, as in the eighteenth century, this public has a virtual monopoly of wealth and influence, then there is no limit to the grossness and inconsequence of the taste which ignorance and arrogance combined will produce.

Of genuine discrimination such a public has none. It wants star singers. Whoever can provide them and their characteristic music is in public estimation a great composer. The most famous composer in the opinion of fashionable Europe in the middle of the eighteenth century bore a name that not one man in a thousand to-day has ever heard of. Bach was a provincial organist, known only to a few scholars, outside his own circle. He died and was forgotten. Handel was a somewhat meteoric genius who chose to exile himself in London and had there failed more than once. A few exceptionally enlightened critics would have pointed to Bach's son Carl as the most gifted master of the future, but the musical public as a whole would have had no sort of doubt as to who was the greatest living musician. His name was Hasse. He had beaten the Italians at their own game, and had done it in Italy. He was a fine singer and player, and he married Faustina Bordoni, a justly celebrated soprano to whom Handel paid two thousand pounds for a London season. 'She is the devil of a singer,' wrote Lady Cowper. Hasse himself was called by the Italians: '*Il caro Sassone*', by others 'the divine Saxon'. This gifted pair were called to direct the opera of the brilliant court at Dresden. There, as in Vienna, London, and the most famous theatres of Italy, the works of Hasse were accounted the finest products of the age.

Hasse was asked to come and supplant Handel in London, but declined. He was the most serious rival to Gluck in Vienna, twenty years later. He wrote more than a hundred operas, and a host of smaller works. He was by common consent the most talented and the most unvaryingly successful musician then alive. In him Italian opera found an inexhaustible fertility which could produce just those songs and just those situations which suited that stage and that public. He lived to the ripe age of eighty-five, having been an acknowledged master for half a century. Yet of all this talent, of all this resounding success, hardly a note remains. So far as permanent musical values are concerned the public opinion of the eighteenth century was wrong, hopelessly and completely wrong. Old Hasse, famous but generous, lived to hear, in 1771, a serenade by Mozart, then a lad of fifteen. 'This boy will cause us all to be forgotten,' said the old man. That sentence is his memorial. He, at any rate, saw further than his public, and is remembered for it.

Much was to happen before the time was ripe for Mozart's maturer work. Italian opera was to be very seriously challenged, and on two sides. The frontal attack was delivered by Gluck, and with him begins the gradual undermining of the Italian ascendancy. A more indirect but in the end a more momentous change was the increasing success of light opera of various kinds, of which a spoken comedy with incidental music was a common type.

Gluck was one of those artists whose work involves not only an intuitive sense of fitness, but also a conscious search for convincing intellectual principles. A gifted child, he approached his musical career in the way which then seemed best to every musician who had the opportunity. He went to Milan, studied hard, and entered the lists as a composer of Italian opera. He had many successes, and was invited to London in 1745. In London he failed, and Handel is reputed to have said of him that 'he had no more counterpoint than his cook'. Failure led him to think out his whole position. He travelled, and wrote other works, many of light and incidental character, but at the same time he devoured languages and literature, pondered over the problems of musical aesthetics, and made many intellectual friends. Ultimately, in 1767, he appeared boldly in Vienna as the convinced apostle of reform. He not only presented operas which openly challenged the whole scheme of Italian dramatic customs, but he wrote reasoned essays to explain his opinions and methods. Here are a few sentences from the preface to his opera 'Alceste':

I have resolved to avoid all those abuses which have crept into Italian opera through the mistaken vanity of singers and the foolish compliance of composers, and which have rendered it wearisome and ridiculous. . . .

I have tried to reduce music to its proper function, that of helping poetry by enhancing the expression of the sentiment. . . .

I have been careful never to interrupt a singer in the heat of a dialogue in order to introduce a tedious refrain, nor to stop him in the middle of a piece either to show the flexibility of his voice or to give him time to take breath for a long-sustained note. . . .

I have not thought it right to hurry through the second part of a song if the words happened to be most important. . . .

The overture ought to indicate the nature of the subject and prepare the audience for the character of the piece they are to see. . . .

These ideals seem to us so reasonable that it is not

easy to realize the shock of surprise and anger they produced. Gluck thus stated his conclusions after long and careful thought. He was in fact returning to the ideals of the first operatic movement in Italy, when Greek drama was the ultimate standard. His contemporaries had strayed so far from that original impulse that they could no longer recognize it. Nor was Gluck a mere theorist. The man who was proposing to put music again under the tutelage of poetic ideas and actions was in fact writing magnificent music, and this music, in its own inherent beauty, was far superior to that of the men who claimed to be so much more faithful to pure music than Gluck's logic would permit. This is the eternal paradox of dramatic inspiration. Those artists who feel reality most keenly are often inspired to write the purest poetry. Those who value poetic form above dramatic truth frequently degenerate into versifiers. Gluck preached musical truth and wrote musical beauty. His rivals worshipped what they held to be beauty and wrote commonplaces.

Vienna was violently critical, but Gluck found there a friend, the French attaché Du Rollet, by whose influence was staged one of the most potent victories in musical history. Gluck set to music the Greek story, in French, of 'Iphigenia in Aulis'. By the help of Du Rollet and the French Queen it was produced in Paris. Whatever men felt about Gluck's theories it was impossible to ignore the depth and sincerity of his dramatic and musical genius. These were real characters, singing with the fervour of truth their real joys and sufferings. The orchestra cast its powerful spell over the scene, now of lyric beauty, now of tragic intensity. Never again could neat inanities pass without challenge. Even Gluck's fiercest critics felt so much.

And critics there were in plenty, beginning with the French Academy of Music. A rival was invited to Paris, the Italian composer Piccinni, who had a just repute in the lighter forms of opera. The quarrel between the two factions was of an extreme bitterness, much more acute than that of the Handel-Buononcini contest in London forty years before. All cultured Paris was either Gluckist or Piccinnist, and the latter party at length reached the crowning folly of inviting Piccinni to reset a libretto which Gluck had already clothed in masterly music. There was a certain superficial fitness in the conditions of the fight. The German Gluck and the Italian Piccinni were competing, as it were, on the neutral soil and in the neutral language of France. But Piccinni was no match for Gluck, and his failure was complete. Yet the contest of wits raged for years afterwards, and it had at least the merit of rousing general European opinion. There is nothing like a pitched literary battle for making men think, and the fierce polemics of the rival parties in Paris did much to educate the best elements in the general public everywhere. A keener attention was secured, not only for Gluck himself, but also for many a later composer who fought under Gluck's standard.

Grand opera was thus given new ideals and a new life. Gluck's classical subjects, treated with a broad and dignified passion, remade the tradition of serious purpose and high argument on the stage. These Greek myths, with their supernatural background, again justified the greatest intensity of dramatic power, and the simple grandeur of Gluck's music kept the whole action on a plane of sincere exaltation. His achievement may be measured by the fact that no operas older than his have held their place in the normal repertory.

Grand opera in the modern theatre virtually begins
with Gluck.

There was, however, another and more general
change in progress, less spectacular than the reforms of
Gluck, but in the end more widespread and permanent.
In London Handel had been beaten by the extravagant
competition of two rival factions for what was essentially one public, the fashionable world. Fashion runs
after one thing at a time. If it prefers Tweedledum,
that is the end of Tweedledee. There are also a good
many sane and ordinary people who welcome something
less pretentious and more amusing than either of the
two. These found what they wanted in 'The Beggar's
Opera', a comedy of low life written by John Gay, and
provided with songs based on all the jolliest tunes
which that astute arranger, Dr. Pepusch, could find.
Here were highwaymen, pickpockets, and their accom-
plices, male and female, caricaturing the well-known
foibles of court and society. Here was a practical skit
on Italian opera, with two rival leading ladies reproducing the feuds notorious among famous operatic singers.
The tunes, popular and traditional, were irresistible.
The venture took London by storm in 1728, and was
repeated all over England. It was the first and most
frank of a long line of musical comedies which threw to
the four winds all the absurdities of Italian grand opera.
It took characters from the streets and taverns, instead
of the incredible gods and heroes of convention, and it
blew a breath of raw but thoroughly fresh air through
the wings of the stage.

The play was in native English, not too nice in verbal
or humorous quality. But though some of its jokes were
broad, it had the merit of making utterly impossible
the strutting and posturing and self-conscious heroics of

K

the foreign operatic star. It offered something vastly
more entertaining than the stale adventures of strange
gods sung in an incomprehensible tongue. It was 'The
Beggar's Opera' which really turned the scale against
Handelian and other importations, and since that time
England has never been without some form of satirical
comedy with incidental music. Most of them have been
a frank hotch-potch of songs and tunes designed to
catch the public ear. They have often been poor in
invention and very ephemeral in taste. But the two
ingredients of keen satire and good tunes have produced
many a typically English mixture. It was just this
combination of talents which Gilbert and Sullivan
raised to the level of a fine art.

From Handel to Sullivan operatic history virtually
ignores England, except as a hunting-ground for fees.
Importations and imitations have been persistent in
season, but chequered in fate. The fact is that since the
puritan revolution we have not been, as a nation,
theatrically minded, still less operatically minded. So
far as opera is concerned the reason is probably in the
main political. Grand opera was essentially an aristocratic art. It needed wealthy and autocratic patronage,
but it also required a special, and in the last resort an
aristocratic, state of mind. The normal deportment of
Louis XIV was that of a stage hero, in private as well
as in public life. It was a perfectly natural expression of
the gulf between him and his subjects. Every princeling
in Europe, for at least two centuries, strove to imitate
him. Their subjects for the most part accepted this
visible attitude of sovereignty as the natural order of
things. What to us is intolerable staginess was to them
the exact representation of heroic and exalted manners.
The English Royal House claimed no such semi-divine

prerogatives, and if our aristocratic societies developed high manners they were yet never without their own keen satirists. Poverty itself could laugh at them without treason. This is why the conventional attitudes and heroics of traditional grand opera have seemed to our public so patently stilted and false. They move us to mirth rather than respect. This is why Gilbert and Sullivan, making fine fun of the pretentious of all kinds, also made the normal educated Englishman feel for the first time really at home in the musical theatre.

We have, of course, no monopoly of this attitude. The Italians themselves felt it, and put it to musical use. While they were busy evolving the forms of serious opera, they were also interpolating between the acts short interludes, or intermezzi, in which dramatic sketches of light or farcical character were given appropriate music. This was the beginning of *opera buffa*, a type of comic opera with spoken dialogue or simple recitative which developed alongside the more ambitious *opera seria*, and proved immensely popular. The French *Opéra Comique* was a related development, not necessarily comic, but invariably spoken, with incidental songs and dances. German *Singspiel* follows the same general lines. All these various offshoots of the more serious musical stage had one feature in common. They were bound by their very nature to use native and comprehensible language. They were thus kept near to a reality of thought and dialect, however overdrawn or farcical they might be in atmosphere. And though for a long time they were considered somewhat beneath the dignity of the most ambitious composers, they at length, by sheer success, attracted the very best talents. They found room for some of the fine natural voices, particularly basses, which grand opera ignored.

They gave a chance to the lighter lyrical talents and to the genuine comedian. Their songs and dances became the favourites of the populace, and as their characters came mainly from the motley crowd of everyday humanity, they made up for any loss of heroic grandeur by a gain in pleasant homeliness and affection. Pergolesi and Cimarosa were both renowned for their operas of this type, and so was Gluck's rival Piccinni.

But the name which in history links superlative music with spoken comedy, and thus draws together the two arts of natural acting and dramatic musicianship, is that of Mozart. The Serenade which Hasse admired was a work of this type. So was 'Il Seraglio'. Of Mozart's later masterpieces it is hardly necessary to speak. 'Figaro', 'The Magic Flute', and 'Don Juan' are incomparable examples of supreme musical craftsmanship combined with intuitive dramatic genius. Mozart commanded everything the Italians had invented and a great deal besides. In particular he took from the *Singspiel* the generous use of duets, trios, quartets, choruses, and all manner of vocal ensembles, which grand opera had found little room for, but which the lighter operas of all schools, Italy included, had made increasingly popular and effective. Nowhere is Mozart's genius more consummate than in this handling of concerted numbers. The individual characters are never lost, yet the texture becomes a kind of vocal chamber-music, perfect in ensemble, and radiant with the added charm of a magical orchestral commentary. It is a return to that combined music-making which has ever been the most fruitful source of the art. It is a definite controlling of the exceptional soloist, whose selfish and thoughtless glorification has so often degraded the stage.

Beethoven's 'Fidelio' also had its dialogue. It is a

noble subject nobly expressed, and falls naturally into the permanent repertory. By the beginning of the nineteenth century Gluck, Mozart, and Beethoven, with some of the more light-hearted Italians, had provided opera with a fine group of masterpieces. That the public too often ran after other and inferior minds is but the natural fate of too mature an excellence. But wherever opera has retained a permanent place in social music, these works have ultimately gained their place in it. They had their own inherent qualities, and they set a standard. They showed how both classical drama and domestic comedy could be clothed in appropriate and lasting music.

5

The eighteenth century came to an end in the midst of violent political upheavals. The American and French Revolutions, and the universal awakening of democratic sentiment of which they were the most vigorous fruits, destroyed at least two of the fundamental assumptions of the previous age. In the Europe of the old régime the nobles were as a whole far more closely linked to their own class, both by intermarriage and by community of interests, than to the peasants and artisans who were their local compatriots and subjects. Even the wars of nations had often been more like family feuds between great houses than clashes of genuine national passion. So great was the social gulf between princes and peoples that it was difficult for them to share the same ideals, and the ruling classes had naturally accepted as inalienable what appeared to be their permanent status in the scheme of things. The reverberations of the French Revolution shattered this complacency, and in spite of its errors and excesses awoke a wide humanitarian fervour. Social and material divisions began to seem less sacred than the common humanity which transcended them. Political agitation and reform was the natural consequence of this change of mind.

But when Napoleon turned reactionary and began to dragoon Europe into his imperial and unified pattern of organization and outlook, it was soon evident that another of the assumptions of the past was dead beyond recall. The ideal of an imperial European unity had survived in theory through all the hundred conflicts which had divided Europe since Rome fell. The Pope in Rome and the Emperor in Vienna had both personified it. The gigantic political plans of Napoleon were to some extent an attempt to revive this old imperial ideal. But the possibility of a real political unity no longer existed, even in the most conservative minds. The very forces which were drawing peoples and nobles into conscious national communities were raising impassable barriers between rival nations. Local patriotisms encouraged in turn keen national ardours. A common language and literature, common traditions and customs, were found to be far stronger than international theories of politics. They were also stronger than the old social order which had made all princes virtually members of one family. Europe awoke to a new ideal, that of an inherent and natural relation between all the members of a race or language, high and low, rich or poor. The political foundations of society became national.

The effect of these ideas on European literature is well understood. There was a like change in some of the features of European music. The growing favour of German *Singspiel* and French *Opéra Comique* was one of the several ways in which national arts began to supplant international fashions. Music did not cease to be, in general, an artistic speech common to the whole of western Europe, but it began to find its deepest sources of inspiration in the emotional tone of a particular locality, of a native language, of a conscious national character. Opera was well fitted to embody these thoughts, because it could give vivid representations of landscape and costume, of the incidents of custom and the interplay of personalities, and it could put these details into a warm setting of speech and song and dance. The young poet Körner, fired by the beauty and passion of German scenes and aspirations, could meet the young musician Weber and inspire him to clothe his lyrics in music equally redolent of those same scenes and traditions. Such songs became a political force as well as an artistic triumph, and when Weber turned to the stage he took with him that professed background of local and national poetry.

The romantic movement of the early nineteenth century is not capable of easy definition, but its main features are as clear in the operas of Weber as in the poetry of Byron and Shelley. Romantic poetry combined a burning interest in the play of human emotions with a keen sense of the mysteries and transcendencies of nature. It sought inspiration in the mountains and rivers, in the fields and woods, in wild and gracious nature, yet kept a warm niche for the adventures of the human spirit, of whatever class or origin. Weber's 'Der Freischütz' is an epitome of these influences. It deals with peasants and huntsmen and sets them in a landscape of field and forest. It is German in speech, in setting, and in music. The call of the hunting horn had been heard through the vast woods of northern

Europe for untold centuries. There is no sound, as there is no instrument, which so moves the hearts of those who live in that environment. Weber depicted a mysterious forest glen, with a spectral and sinister hunter who could help men to forge magic weapons of the chase. There is also a humble romance which, after tragic uncertainties, issues in the triumph of virtue and the death of the tempter. There are peasant dances, romantic songs, and a whole series of wonderful orchestral pictures. Weber's sense of orchestral colour was exceptionally vivid. He was saturated with the inflexions of national melodies. He took the hunting-horn and made its characteristic notes into themes and tunes. It is no wonder that his opera was hailed almost as the birth of a nation. It put on the stage and into music just what every ardent listener then felt most deeply. It was love and home and religion and nation-hood, all cemented into one artistic whole.

Since that time local and national themes have found their natural home on the stage, in every country and in every language. There have been many such borrowed subjects too. Rossini wrote 'William Tell', Auber 'Masaniello'. Verdi, by a remarkable coincidence between native genius and a surrounding political ferment, became a synonym for the Italian Risorgimento. Men chalked his name in the streets, for it also signified *Vittorio Emanuele, Re D'Italia*.

Verdi and Wagner were born in the same year, 1813. Both lived to a ripe age, and both devoted all their talents to the theatre. Both reached world-wide fame. If the dramatic ideals of the nineteenth century are to be found anywhere, they should be clear in the work of these two outstanding men. Verdi was of peasant stock, with a strong simple character, a distrust of theories, and a healthy contempt for all forms of artistic affectation. He felt intensely every situation involving human passions, but he felt it without any desire to theorize upon it. Tragedy or comedy, romance or farce, all found sympathy in him, provided he could bring them within his own dramatic intuitions and clothe them with direct musical expression. It is this directness of Verdi which surprises, and at times antagonizes, the minds of subtler and more introspective artists. He is always frankly inside his characters. He is never writing about himself.

One of the weaknesses of the romantic movement was the tendency of some artists, poets, painters and musicians alike, as well as writers of prose romance, to put themselves and their own personal reactions too clearly in the middle of every picture. In portraying nature they were apt to dwell mainly on the analysis of their own external moods. In depicting human character they were inclined to indulge in personal confessions, in descriptions of their own prevailing sympathies, probing their own souls rather than seeking genuinely to encompass the minds of others. Verdi was totally incapable of this anxious and exaggerated introspection. His temperament was above all things generous and receptive, and he openly and humbly sought to write music which all men might find infectious and beautiful. He further belonged to a country where opera was so integral a part of social life that it had something of the nature of a skilled craft, varying greatly in quality, but not normally involving either the ardours of propaganda or the solemnity of prophecy. Dozens of new operas were written in Italy every year. Thousands of singers and players had no other occupation. The whole public, rich and poor alike, supported opera with no more special concern than they would give to the reading of a book or the view of a picture. It was a part of their daily life, and they accepted it as such.

Verdi, like his Italian folk, was objective, open-hearted, frank. Even in the Manzoni Requiem he does not describe the sorrows of Verdi, but the tragedy and pains of death. And these are real fears, not spiritual allegories. On the stage his method is the same. He will seek the most direct means of inspiring his singers to lose themselves in their parts, just as he himself has given his whole mind and heart to the drama, for its own sake; and he wants his audience to find his music equally fitting and clear and infectious.

The social changes of the century had already brought every suitable subject within the range of the stage, in Italy as elsewhere. For Verdi there was the added spice that any line which could possibly be interpreted as a tilt at the Austrian domination of Italy was sure of a rapturous welcome. Yet in regard both to this and to all the other problems of artistic conduct, Verdi never allowed himself to preach. If politics came into his plot, then he was ready to underline them. But he was equally ready to forget every social and aesthetic pre-occupation of the time, and write melodies which made men forget the very existence of a political or intellectual world. That was his gift and that his appeal. He could dramatize as clearly by touches of orchestration as by contrast of parts, by the surges of a simple chorus as by the masterly handling of elaborate situations. But the surpassing feature of all his most popular works were those quite formal yet quite irresistible Italian tunes which flowed so spontaneously from his pen, and which every one in the theatre began to hum next day. Indeed the whole world hummed them, Vienna, Dresden, Paris, London, Buenos Ayres, and New York. The singers were inspired, the audiences enraptured, and a hundred opera-houses found themselves almost solvent. How different it was from that odd stuff which was coming from Germany, which nobody could sing, and which was unintelligible when sung!

Wagner belonged to the educated middle class, the true heirs of the nineteenth century. He had in his blood traces of the competent civil servant, whose failing is often a certain administrative arrogance, a lack of patience with fools. Wagner was well educated, and educated himself further to a very high intellectual distinction. His early life, through his step-father, the actor and playwright Geyer, made him familiar with the stage. Weber visited his home, and was the object of the young Wagner's deepest reverence. He read Greek and Latin, wrote Shakespearian tragedy, studied philosophy and aesthetics, and knew 'Der Freischütz' by heart. His early music is curiously undistinguished. He was, in fact, one of those artists who become great not by spontaneous gift, but by intense and prolonged thought. Opera was his ambition, but he approached it with a mind full of ideas totally outside the range of the popular products of his time.

Gluck, Mozart, and Weber had lived, but these were not yet the accepted classics of the theatre. Even when Wagner, after many vicissitudes, at length became conductor of the opera at Dresden in 1843, there was some uncertainty as to whether he should rank with the conductor in charge of the Italian repertory. And this repertory was of course pre-Verdi. Wagner's achievements as a conductor lay precisely in his devoted productions of Gluck, Mozart, Beethoven, and Weber, productions at that time unique in their care and insight. However original his own creations were to be, he had at least a first-hand knowledge of the risks and difficulties of operatic administration, and he had given unstinted pains and energy to securing the finest possible interpretations of the works in which he believed.

As a composer Wagner found himself driven towards reforms more drastic than any which had yet been attempted. He saw far beyond Gluck. A language other than his own was of course unthinkable for his purpose, but he went the whole length of devising his own subjects, planning his own dramatic handling, and writing his own verse. Any dramas other than the most artistically exalted were equally distasteful to him, and he wanted not only a complete native and romantic folk-lore, but a comprehensive mythology as well, and this not of Greece but of his own more northern ancestry. He had a whole philosophy to instil, as well as a story to unfold. The impulse behind Wagner's work is a vision of the theatre as a mirror of the whole material, intellectual, and spiritual world, a mirror reflecting not only human passions and achievements, but also showing the ultimate and divine order of the universe.

'The Flying Dutchman', 'Tannhäuser', and 'Lohengrin' were romantic operas, all closely connected with northern legend and folk-lore. Both in method and interpretation they made the greatest possible demands on the technical and artistic resources of the theatre as it then existed, and Wagner would permit no abatement of his elaborate ordering of detail. These works had to be done properly, or not at all. Then, after some years at Dresden, he found himself proclaimed as a

friend of the political revolutions which centred round
the year 1848, and in 1849 he had to leave his post and
face a long exile. He had no sure means of subsistence
and no certain artistic prospects, and it was under these
formidable shadows that he gave such proofs of artistic
power and will as must remain for all time the wonder
of every dramatic and musical chronicler. By a supreme
act of faith he deliberately devoted the best years of his
life to the inception and gradual completion of a work
of colossal proportions, a work covering the whole
range of his ideas, philosophic, poetic, and musical, and
a work which he, the practical operatic producer, of
all men well knew to be absolutely beyond the available
means of any theatre then existing in the world. There
is in music no parallel to 'The Ring'. There is no
parallel to it in any other art. If an architect were to
spend half his life designing a huge and elaborate
building which was not only unauthorized and un-
wanted, but for which the very materials did not at the
time exist anywhere in the world, that would be a fair
parallel to Wagner's chosen task.

It was precisely this same unbending force of character which turned Europe into an arena of Wagnerian
controversy. A combination of sublime faith, inflexible
will, practical idealism, and a genius that could trans-
mute the most forbidding and intractable subjects into
glorious and original music, was strong enough to defy
fate itself. Wagner made opera into a religion. His
disciples were driven to worship, his detractors to fury.
For his detailed technique was just as uncompromising
as his choice of ideas. His most impressionable years
had been spent in studying and producing the symphonies of Beethoven, of which he had given performances unique in their care and devotion. His conception

of opera was of an extended and dramatic symphony, developing with slow but irresistible force the emotional essence of a prophetic story. Musically, he put this gradual unfolding of atmosphere not so much on the stage as in the orchestra. The singers were in the main to declaim their words. Only in moments of lyric rapture would he permit a formal melody. The singers were to be one, and only one, of the many threads in an elaborate texture of sound, and even the most pregnant melodic themes were as a rule denied them, the orchestra being the predominant partner throughout. The ablest and most sympathetic singers said their parts were unsingable. Wagner made them learn a new method. The orchestral players said Wagner had written beyond the capacities of their instruments and of their skill. Wagner made them strive to do better. The producers said his scenic effects were outside practical stage mechanics. Wagner made them rebuild their theatres.

Nor did he confine himself to the stage. It was impossible to follow a tithe of Wagner's concentrated musical thought unless the performance could be heard without interruption or distraction. Wagner made the audience arrive in time for the first note and sit quiet till the last. However strong the desire and habit of giving some expression to their views and feelings, by applause or otherwise, Wagner made them bow to his will. There were intervals at the end of every hour or so. Then, or never, the audience might show its existence. From the entry of the conductor to the fall of the curtain, and even after the fall, if the orchestra still had something to add, Wagner made men listen as no audience had ever listened before, outside a religious service. Indeed the first and greatest Wagnerian theatre can only be described in semi-religious terms. A miracle happened. Ludwig of Bavaria gave Wagner a refuge and helped him to build an opera-house conceived in every detail for the production of 'The Ring'. It was not bricks and mortar only, but a whole setting, a temple, a cult. People came from the ends of the earth to Bayreuth, an obscure little town hitherto unknown, and there they completely surrendered themselves to the aesthetic and intellectual power of this astonishing man. They lodged where he told them. They took their meals at his convenience. They sat through long hours of his complicated music without a murmur, absorbed, hypnotized. The finest conductors, singers, and players counted it an honour to be asked to take whatever part Wagner might be pleased to give them in this unique ritual. He ruled them all equally, with an iron hand. It was the Oracle of Delphi returned to earth.

And he gave no quarter to any one. Not a song, not a dance; not a duet or chorus, except as strictly germane to the drama. His verse was consciously archaic in mood, full of the crude alliterations, the forced assonances, and the tortuous descriptions of Norse saga. No plain statement was ever made if it could be couched in prophecy instead. There were long passages of philosophic disquisition and dispute. His actors were either incarnations of pagan heroisms or grim potentialities and powers, gods of the northern fires and forests. His staging was frank realism, thunder and lightning, winds and storms, clouds and torrents, giants, gnomes, dragons, birds, magic swords and armour, spells, potions, dooms, and oracles. No humour, no wit, beyond an occasional sardonic and heavy-footed jest. This was grand opera indeed, grand opera with a vengeance, as uncompromising an embodiment of artistic purpose as the world had ever seen. And there in his shrine, the house 'Wahnfried', and in his fine clothes, lived Wagner, the prophet of a new evangel, secure at last in the ardent homage of the faithful.

The Bayreuth project had had the support of many Wagner societies in all parts of the world, and the cult of 'The Ring' at length reached every artistic centre which could hope to produce it. Much of the atmosphere of Bayreuth went with it. Men shut up their shops and closed their offices to go to the Wagner opera. It was no light and casual entertainment after a hard day's work, but a severe and disciplined aesthetic education. If our social historians ever deign to observe such things, they will have to give a chapter to Wagner as an influence on public manners. In the theatre, and indirectly in the concert-hall, he enforced a new standard of attention, a new habit of demeanour. The solemnity and decorum which now so generally distinguishes our public musical deportment is in very substantial measure due to Wagner and the Wagnerian cult.

'The Ring' is Wagner, but by no means the whole Wagner. He could also create 'The Mastersingers', a charming comedy of art, as melodious and fragrant and romantic as a medieval garland. 'Tristan' is an intense analysis of the power and tragedy of erotic passion. 'Parsifal' puts into music the incense of religion. The genius of Wagner was almost universal in its range, and wherever he projected his thought he said something extraordinarily original and pregnant. It is in fact this distinction and concentration of sheer musical power which has carried the whole fabric of Wagnerian drama on its back. Had he been less gifted

as a musician his grandiose plans would have seemed to
be the mere vapourings of a crank. It was his music
which conquered both the distrustful and the lukewarm.
No man was ever more fiercely criticized. Any one who
has given a moment's thought to the subject finds that
all drama is a compromise, music-drama a logical
contradiction. Wagner's overbearing confidence, his
ruthless argument, his artistic bad manners, not to
mention a good many private failings which were no
secret either to friends or foes, made him a proper
target for the shafts of those who felt the beauty or
serenity of other ideals. An art more elusive and less
polemical might yet have its own charm and its own
real value. An old-fashioned story decked with old-
fashioned tunes might not explain the genesis of the
universe, but it might fill men with emotions for which
they felt no need to apologize. Yet when men left off
arguing and turned to Wagner's music, his themes, his
harmonies, his marvellous architecture of sound, then
the tumult gradually ceased, and the whole world
began to share the wonder of those first friends who had
heard snatches of this music long before, when Wagner
was still in process of creating it, when his name was as
yet clouded, and when there seemed no possible chance
that his great projects would ever be more than a
hopeless dream.

6

The opposition to Wagner was not all of it captious.
There were critics who both grasped his ideas and felt
the power of his music, yet refused to be carried off
their feet by what they held to be a personal rather than
a universal method of expression. Art has room for all
temperaments, for all moods, and only a minority are

L

Wagnerian by instinct. The Italians went on writing their tunes, Wagner or no Wagner, but they learnt a great deal from his dramatic continuity of method, and they helped themselves liberally from his orchestral palette. The French, who had been very slow indeed to admit any virtue at all in the mature Wagner, pursued their own aims, good and bad, without much reference to what came from beyond the Rhine. They liked a lavish spectacle, they liked well-constructed scenes of sentiment or passion, they liked a sparkling ballet. If the musical counterpart of these things was a little shallow, it was at least neat and competent. French grand opera continued, and some of its successes were welcomed even in Germany. The most notable contribution of France to the enlargement of operatic technique came neither from its own nor from any other of the traditional grand manners. A small group of impressionist artists and poets found in Debussy a musical colleague. Debussy scorned alike the thin brilliance of Paris and the solemn pomp of Wagner. With deliberate elusiveness and refinement, ignoring all the formal traditions both of melody and harmony, Debussy invested Maeterlinck's story of 'Pelléas et Mélisande' with a new and remarkably subtle background of musical suggestion. The stage had rarely been accompanied with such reticence, with such an original and delicate film of harmonic and orchestral colour, and if there was a lack of the warmer and more solid tints, there was also a welcome absence of exaggeration and emphasis. Those who flinched at the sledge-hammer blows of Wagner and his pupils could find an art still more novel, yet cool and imaginative, in the gentle strokes of Debussy.

Meanwhile the exploitation of national idioms and

local colours went on apace, particularly in Bohemia,
in Hungary, and in Spain. It was Spain that influenced
France, rather than Germany, for more than half of
France looks south, and prefers Spanish dances to
Teutonic sermons. But the operatic school which at
length forced itself into decided prominence was that
which two generations of intense national endeavour had
brought to life in Russia. Here were melodies of vivid
local atmosphere, fine dramatic intuitions, rich orchestration, barbaric splendour of scene and subject,
prodigies of heroism and endurance, and a remarkably
original instinct for the management of crowds. The
blazing cauldron of Russian politics, the number and
variety of her human types, the strong mixture of
oriental and savage blood, the complete candour of her
stage temper and mood, all these found a place in
Russian opera and came to Western Europe with the
force of a new discovery. The most astonishing triumphs
were in the direction of ballet, whether conceived as
part of the dramatic use and control of large numbers of
people in social action, which could thus make the stage
chorus extraordinarily significant and effective, or
developed as a separate and self-sufficing spectacle,
presenting what was to Western eyes a new art of the
stage.

The Russian ballet rested on the splendour and resources of the Russian Imperial court, a society possessing most of the amenities of Western civilization, yet
not many generations removed from barbarism. Careful recruiting, long training, and iron discipline had
made the Russian *corps de ballet* an instrument with
which genius could do anything. The telling of a story,
the expression of a mood, the delineation of passion and
adventure could be achieved with hardly less clarity

than words could give, certainly with a likeness far more vivid than the half-heard verses of a song. In sheer beauty and complexity of gesture no singer could compete with the trained dancer, and an unlimited range of figures and costumes offered no unworthy parallel to the kaleidoscope of life. Opera had already learnt, as we have seen, to put the greater part of its musical thought into the orchestra, rather than into the declamation of its singers. Could not this same orchestral expressiveness be used to give all the musical commentary necessary to enhance the unfolding of a living picture on the stage? This the Russian ballet did, and composers of dramatic talent were greatly attracted by the prospect of being able to say all they would in purely orchestral terms.

There was no longer any problem of vocal balance, and this was a great gain in general musical freedom. Further, the musicianship of orchestral players was as a rule much better than that of any but the best operatic singers. And the orchestra could be used as a medium complete in itself, handicapped by none but its own internal and comparative values. Dancers and ballet-masters of the Russian standard asked for nothing better than an opportunity to express by gesture and movement the outline of a dramatic or lyric situation, helped by the rich undercurrent of melody, harmony, colour, and lilt which a symphonic orchestra could so effectively supply. This type of dramatic ballet would have been much less convincing had not Wagner already completed the subservience of formal designs to the necessities of dramatic action. It would also have been very narrow in range without the great wealth of dramatic associations which had become common to all stage music. Given these antecedents, the composer of dramatic ballet had few limits to his devices of expression. All the accepted dramatic elements in music were there in vast number, and if imagination could invent a new dynamic or emotional suggestion, then a quick-witted dancer and an expectant audience would soon guess its meaning.

Every country is now imitating this art of dramatic dancing which Russian technique has made so wide in resource and interpretation. It seems as if ballet of this kind will henceforth hold a serious and independent place in the theatre. Spectacular ballet has always existed since the stage began. It was an offshoot of elaborate ritual. It gathered to itself all the steps and figures of formal dancing, and added to these the active wit and drollery of the carnival. Last but by no means least, it discovered the very real pathos of dumb show. Punch and Judy and the dog Toby have ever delighted the young in spirit of all ages. The art of the marionette can be so handled that its delicate fancifulness becomes a convincing epitome of life's most moving characters and encounters. Imagination thrives on limitations. The artistic sense becomes the more acute as it is more concentrated in aim. A living puppet can draw from us our intuitive sympathy with inarticulate emotion, and can also show us either the wayward clumsiness or the controlled grace of all animate things. Dramatic ballet has realized these possibilities, these expressive facets of the human mind and heart. It came at a time when the silent portrayal of scenes and emotions, the art of the cinematograph, was rapidly becoming the most popular entertainment in the world. That art too had its accompanying music, though it never got beyond the broadest appeals to sentiment and rough realism of association. All the conditions were against restraint and subtlety. A heterogeneous public asks of music only the most direct and obvious allusions.

But in dramatic ballet proper there is room for the keenest shafts of musical thought. There is even room for the music of the concert-hall. Men have written ballet for music as freely as music for ballet. The foundations of both lie in the steadily growing appreciation of purely instrumental musical speech. Voices are no longer essential, even on the stage. The orchestra is now our most characteristic medium of expression, with or without voices as an adjunct. Indeed the voices themselves are not infrequently used as subsidiary orchestral instruments, rather than as personal and individual soloists of especial status. It is a curious end to three centuries of development. That old paradise of the singer, the conventional opera-house, has gradually transferred its most important musical thoughts from the stage to the orchestra. The first great step, from lyric song to vocal drama, turned singing into declamation. The last step, from music-drama to dramatic ballet, reduces the singer to silence.

THE CONCERT-HALL

THE CONCERT-HALL

I

IN a narrow street in Oxford, named perhaps after a once Holy Well, there is a music-room which claims to be the oldest public concert-hall in Europe. It was opened in 1748. Handel is said to have visited it, Haydn conducted his works there, and it has probably heard as much fine music and as many fine musicians as any place of its size in the world. It is quite small, seating about three hundred people comfortably, with a semi-circular end-wall bounding a platform on which fifty performers would be somewhat closely packed. It is an interesting survival of what was then considered an adequate scale for public performances of concerted music. It reminds us that Bach could produce a work like the St. Matthew Passion, including its two complete choruses and orchestras, with about half a hundred performers all told. It tells us that the first public concert-halls were hardly larger than a spacious draw-ing-room, just as the public Assembly Rooms of fashionable spas were not greatly different from the reception rooms of a large town house. The first public audiences were in fact of the same select social class as those who heard Louis XIV's 'twenty-four violins' at Versailles, or Frederick the Great's flute concertos at Potsdam. An announcement in the fashionable Intel-ligence, a high price of subscription, a small band of performers, and an audience who were for the most part mutually acquainted, these were the usual conditions of a public concert. We should be inclined to call it chamber music, not unlike the kind of musical party given from time to time by a musical club.

There was in fact no essential difference between the musical recreations of great houses and the earliest public concerts. Players, singers, and programmes were largely fluid. There might be solos, duets, trios, concertos, choruses, and symphonies given in quite casual order in the same programme. The orchestra came in the main from the theatre, a very few players to each part, with a sprinkling of distinguished leaders. The chorus usually came from a neighbouring church or cathedral, but choral performances outside church or theatre were then rare. Distinguished singers, distinguished players, and a few concerted items were the usual features of a concert. The whole atmosphere was far more intimate and personal, the standard of performance more casual, than we are now accustomed to in public. The concertos of Bach and Handel, and those of scores of their forgotten contemporaries, all admitting wide variations of numbers and instruments, are characteristic. Every performance, and nearly every concerted work, was a special event prepared for special conditions.

The music was almost entirely contemporary, often written for the occasion by the player-composers who were present. There was no library to draw on, no music shops, very few printed works, and these generally in score or in a keyboard arrangement. The parts had to be copied, and there was no permanent organization. The standard of performance was from our point of view very rough and ready. There was no specialist conductor. The composer usually sat at the harpsichord or organ and filled in harmonies as he wished. The leading violin gave beats with his bow, or tapped the time on his desk, or stamped his foot. There was little detailed variation or careful balance of tone. Passages were in the main either loud or soft. Solo-playing was of course expressive and distinctly phrased, but for the mass of players the most typical effects were those of strong contrasts, echoes, and the like. What we now achieve by a disciplined crescendo or by a gradual diminution of sound was hardly thought of. Variety was chiefly obtained by varied use of the number of players. The harpsichord alone, with string basses, or with a flute or violin solo, were typical accompaniments for a solo voice. The music might constantly veer between solo passages, chamber music, and full orchestral or choral effects.

The audience was free in its manners and firmly convinced of the accuracy and value of its opinions. It made no secret of its desire to be interested and pleased. It did not come to be educated, and brooked no dull artistic sermons. The arbiters of skill and intelligence were in the audience, not on the platform. Surprise and delight were the emotions most in vogue, surprise at a new dexterity, delight in a warm tone or in a taking phrase. Pathos was in demand, but not too crude, not too direct. The portrayal of a refined and somewhat self-conscious passion by means of vocal artifices was greatly favoured. It was the age of the virtuosi, narrow in emotional range, but very progressive in technical skill. As yet the players were not nearly so specialized as the singers, but they were fast improving.

When Corelli's violin sonatas were first taken to Paris, no one could play them. Only the trained singers could master such parts at that time. It was not until the middle of the eighteenth century that solo instrumental performers could compete in public favour with the trained voice. The keyboard had developed a high standard, as Handel, Domenico Scarlatti, and of course Bach and his pupils, bear proof, but that was largely because the harpsichord fulfilled more than a solo function. It played through everything, and was incessantly practised. The violin was in the infancy of its technique. Players had not even discovered the most convenient way to hold it. It was held on what is now the wrong side of the tail piece, and this made the higher positions almost impossible for the left hand. In 1740 an Italian violinist, Geminiani, published an instruction-book advocating the better way of holding the violin. He visited London, and it is recorded that his method enabled him to play with ease passages which were thought to be impossibly difficult. It was in 1756 that Mozart's father, Leopold, issued his *Violin-School*, which became the best known of all violin manuals. These books were symptomatic of the growing prestige of the violin as a solo instrument. Its progress was henceforth very rapid, and each advance passed down from master to pupil. There is no finer musical genealogy than the great chains of violinists, masters, and pupils, of which at least one direct line, from Corelli through Somis, Pugnani, Viotti, Rode, and Böhm, at length reaches Joachim and the players of our own time. In the middle of the eighteenth century Tartini was the reigning genius, though he held to the old methods and his works are by modern standards technically easy. Early in the nineteenth century Paganini carried the execution of acrobatics on the violin to such a pitch of skill that his contemporaries said he was bewitched, and the best players of to-day are well content if they can get so far.

The music which some of these men wrote and played was of little permanent worth, but their dexterity attracted the favour of the public and accustomed men's ears to ranges of sound which greatly extended the vocabulary of music. And there is no technical device, however barren of artistic value initially, which does not sooner or later meet a composer who can give it perspective and distinction. The whole literature of solo concertos has arisen because there were players of outstanding power and brilliance who could fill a position of special prominence. All composers have found in the superlative playing of specialists a fertile source of encouragement and inspiration. To combine such powers with the rich colours of an orchestra has served both composers and listeners equally well. The audience may, if it will, admire the skill of its favourite, while the musician can enjoy the delicate balance and interplay of the whole fabric.

The concerto presents an outline of the technical history of orchestral music. An exceptional player commands what is for his generation a rare power over his instrument. His achievement becomes the normal standard of a later time. Players again go further and make a new standard, and so on. Any competent orchestral player to-day has a technique in many respects far beyond the utmost conceptions of his predecessors of two centuries ago. The concerto is a memorial of this individual distinction as it was evolved step by step, and as it was passed on gradually to all trained players. One feature, the cadenza, gave the soloist a chance of showing his particular powers, either of temperament or method. As in the solo part as a whole he stood out from the rank and file, so in the cadenza he was expected to demonstrate his own imagination and skill as compared with other soloists of distinction. The cadenza survives from the time when extemporary playing was an essential accomplishment of all players of the first rank, when every player was to this extent a composer too. The earliest concertos have as a rule no cadenza. They are concerted pieces using one or two comparatively specialized players. Concertos written for the virtuoso proper included a cadenza and left it to the fancy of the player. Modern concertos either have no cadenza or give it in fixed and written form. That is the history of instrumental technique. The individual discovered it and at first did as he pleased. Later it became a normal standard and was made subject to orchestral discipline. That done, the time was ripe for the orchestral symphony as such, in its own right. The symphony is a concourse of players who are all experts, but all made to serve a common and greater end.

This gradual development of technical skill was the foundation of the concert music which was eventually to occupy so paramount a place in the progress of pure music, but there were many other features of eighteenth-century music, some social, some accidental, which played an important part in developing both the performers and the public taste on which in the end all improvement must depend. One most characteristic fashion was the provision of all kinds of entertainment, including music, in public pleasure-gardens, or in buildings which were designed as much for social intercourse as for the incidental arts which shared a place in them. The Rotunda opened in the Ranelagh gardens in 1742, for example, was an odd mixture of social and artistic purposes. The orchestra occupied the middle of the floor. Around it was a wide promenade where the public could see and be seen. The walls of the building were tiers of boxes in which small parties could eat and drink and converse. It was an arena, a theatre, a concert-room, and a social meeting-place all in one. More popular still were the famous gardens at

Vauxhall, which for over a century attracted the London public by entertainments of all kinds.

The nearest modern parallel to the Vauxhall of eighteenth-century London is the Crystal Palace at Sydenham, which was in fact opened just about the time that Vauxhall finally disappeared. Vauxhall had its pleasure-gardens, its menagerie, its fireworks, its tight-rope walkers. It had a fine organ specially built for solo and concerted use, and organ concertos were for a long time an invariable feature of its concerts. It engaged the most famous singers and players; it had of course an orchestra and sometimes a chorus as well. An astute manager in 1749 contrived to hold there the rehearsals of Handel's music celebrating the peace of Aix-la-Chapelle. Twelve thousand people came to hear it, and London Bridge, then the only one, was blocked for hours. Later Vauxhall housed a ballet, a vaudeville troupe, and a circus. These gardens were intended to supply a growing need, due to rapid and prosperous urban development, for places where large numbers of people of all but the poorest classes could find recreation. Their place is now mainly taken by the lighter sorts of public music, by hotels, restaurants, tea-shops, and picture-houses. Vauxhall had at times a very dubious moral atmosphere, and there was much excessive eating and drinking, but there were practically no other places of entertainment suitable for family parties and large numbers, and the garden therefore attracted this public and based its varied side-shows on this patronage. A century later the Crystal Palace showed what could be done for good music in such surroundings, given enlightened direction. A wind band was enlarged into a permanent orchestra, and for many years the Crystal Palace concerts were among the best and most enterprising in Europe. They led the way for that general musical activity which is now shown by all progressive health and holiday resorts.

In the eighteenth century such pleasure-gardens were to be found in most of the capital cities of Europe, and one of them, the Augarten in Vienna, is remembered for some exceptionally fruitful performances. It was there, from 1782 onwards, that Mozart and his works were frequently heard, as were the symphonies of Beethoven later   One curious début deserves special record, both as a sidelight on the customs of that time and place, and as an odd fact in musical history. The concerts in the Augarten were given at the peculiarly inartistic time, as we should think, of seven-thirty in the morning. The early walk or drive, the semi-open-air conditions of performance, and the fresh and rural atmosphere clearly appealed to a large number of the residents of Vienna's old and crowded streets. On one particular Thursday morning in May 1803 a first performance of unusual character was given. The violinist was a mulatto, Bridgetower by name, and a fine player, but so extravagant in his manner that people laughed while they listened. The pianist was Beethoven, and together they played from a manuscript hardly dry. That manuscript was the 'Kreutzer' Sonata. One wonders what the audience thought of it, how many of them could have had a suspicion that this work would one day be the most famed of all sonatas for the violin. And one wonders too whether it is equally possible that in some such incongruous environment to-day, as we might think, in some hotel lounge or municipal bandstand, there is being played a new work which will also have its special paragraph in the records of the art, a century hence.

Another characteristic feature of eighteenth-century social life also had its due effect on music. Practically the only places which were tolerably convenient for a men's social club were the taverns and coffee-houses. Many of these are famous in literature, and they were the forerunners of all the later artistic, professional, and political clubs. These taverns had their music, and the most popular of them grew into the public music-halls of the nineteenth century. Some of the old customs long survived. Members elected a chairman in rotation, who sat at the head of the table and called for songs all round. This practice of appointing officers or members in turn to choose the programmes was kept up by far more ambitious societies, like those of the famous Ancient Concerts. The informal concert of the tavern has its place in history and leads without a break to the variety theatre of modern times.

More important in a musical sense were the Glee and Catch clubs which had met informally long before they took to a definite organization. In the later eighteenth century such male voice clubs became very numerous, and in many cases well specialized. In Germany they were a social and political force, they eventually supported an extensive musical literature, and they paved the way for the innumerable male voice choirs of colleges, clubs, and barracks, where natural musical instincts can be fortified by the team-spirit. The English glee clubs which flourished towards the end of the century were excellent training grounds for amateur singers, and as soon as social custom allowed women also to take their share in important choral organizations, the large mixed chorus was ready for its work.

M

2

In 1738, about ten years before the opening of the Holywell music-room, Handel had given a benefit concert in London which brought him a thousand pounds and cleared him of debt. This event may have encouraged him to leave the speculative enterprises of the opera-house and write music for concert performance instead of for the stage. The underlying character of the music did not altogether change, but instead of being made subservient to a conventional libretto, to extravagant costumes and machinery, and to all the personal whims and rivalries inseparably connected with operatic performers and audiences at that time, he could choose his own subjects, could use soloists, chorus, and orchestra with dramatic freedom, and even if such a work had only a meagre success, it did not involve complete bankruptcy. He turned to the epic stories of the Bible, then as now an unfailing source of inspiration to the most solid strata of the English people, and by clothing these stories with the fine dramatic and musical emphasis of which he had so remarkable a command, he led his own mind and that of his English public into the artistic channel which has proved to be of all others the most congenial and permanent.

Handel offered overtures, recitative, solos, and choruses, lyric and dramatic, contemplative and descriptive, allied to religious words and origins deep in the instincts of his audience and divorced from the tawdry and superficial temptations of the stage. There were no expensive mechanics, vying with each other in ingenuity. There were no capering singers, intent only on fees and limelight. There was even a comparatively disciplined public which, whatever its tastes in music, paid an

intuitive homage to an impressive and sacred theme.
'Saul' and 'Israel in Egypt' were produced in 1739.
'The Messiah' was written in twenty-three days in 1741,
and sung in Dublin in 1742. It came to London the
next year, but was held for a time to be inferior to
'Samson'. Not till 1750 did it begin to make for itself
its unique place in English music. Meanwhile Handel
had again suffered much by the fickleness of his public,
had been again bankrupt, and again broken in health.
But he had inaugurated a musical development of the
first quality, which was to spread at length throughout
the whole English-speaking world. He had produced
an unparalleled wealth of music which could minister
to at least two of our ruling passions, our reverence for
the English Bible and our delight in choral singing.
Giraldus in the twelfth century had noted our love
of part-singing. Six hundred years later we were, in this
respect at least, still true to tradition. This it was
which made Handel an English composer, in spite of
his foreign birth.

Beethoven was by extraction a Fleming, Haydn a
Croat, but both belong by virtue of their lives and works
to Vienna, and no one would question the fact. So the
Handel oratorio belongs to England, and it would be
perverse pedantry to say that an art which has so fundamentally captured and held the sustained artistic
convictions of a whole nation, for generation after
generation, is an exotic and foreign thing. The geo-
graphy of music consists not in the places where
musicians are born, but in the places where music is
lived. The two may coincide or not, as chance favours or
rejects a particular talent. We have made Handel into
an Englishman by choosing and accepting his music as
our principal heritage. We did this because we found

in it qualities intuitively felt to be congenial. The most rigorous test of nationality can do no more. In earlier years Handel had written German oratorio in Germany, and Italian oratorio in Italy. His English oratorios were a far more distinguished product of his genius, and they belong to our soil.

The first, 'Esther', performed in the chapel of the Duke of Chandos in 1720, has a special interest because it was written when the old connexion between oratorio and the stage had not entirely ceased. In 1731 the Children of the King's Chapel performed it with costumes and scenery, and so did another company, without Handel's consent. Handel thereupon produced it himself 'By His Majesty's Command', but without action, at the King's Theatre in 1732. He had yet to suffer much in his pursuit of operatic success, and had yet to retire from that ruinous public rivalry which destroyed both his fortune and his health, but he had shown that oratorio, in concert form, could employ the full measure of his talents, and he ultimately turned to it for good. It is a significant fact in the history of the period that the sheer prestige of Italian opera should for so long have obsessed his mind, and this in spite of constant difficulties and disappointments. He was a child of his age. He may almost be said to have written oratorios in spite of himself, so strong was the lure of the stage. Yet the stage, to all intents, had no place for a chorus, and if there is one talent more than another which is inseparably identified with Handel, it is the superb ease and mastery of his choral instinct. It was this choral power which marked his English oratorios from the first. It was this which has endeared them to every singer in England. There is a pathos in the story of this man, already growing old and stricken in health and fortune, turning at long last to the less spectacular, less fashionable, but infinitely more enduring work which occupied his later creative years.

Not that he could have had the smallest premonition of the degree to which his sacred music would be cherished, or of the steps by which it grew to be so characteristically native an art. When we think of typical Handelian effects, of massive numbers and broad generalizations of style, we are recalling occasions and resources of which Handel himself can have had no conception. He used all the material available in his day, but this was by modern standards very restricted, and with him only less than with Bach is it true that we have turned an art written for special and narrower circumstances into the vehicle of our most corporate and public expressions of artistic faith. The shock Handel would receive if he could return to hear one of our massive performances of his work would be exactly equalled by our own surprise, if we could reverse the years and hear one of his oratorios as he imagined and performed them.

In the first place, there were no women in the choirs of Handel's time. Handel's chorus was a chorus of men and boys. Only later in the century, and after his death, did women begin to occupy what seems to us to be their obvious and natural place in a large chorus. The Church had always frowned on women's voices. This was part of the long monastic tradition of segregation and asceticism, but it was also in keeping with many fundamental and secular social instincts. Women were out of place in public life, except in the rare circumstances of a special birthright. They might sing in a convent and control their own private religious offices there, but they had no share in the public worship of the

Church, except as members of the general congregation. And the stage was for centuries equally closed to them. Shakespeare's heroines were impersonated by boys, and the opinion that the stage was not the place for a self-respecting woman, an opinion often in full accord with the facts, persisted long after the theatre had largely purged itself of its more dubious associations. It was the clear superiority of women's soprano voices which first brought them into the theatre, but the innovation was only gradually accepted, and even Lulli had thought it worth while to get special and official authorization for his use of women singers. Handel of course employed women as soloists, both in the theatre and in oratorio, but his oratorio choir was essentially a church choir, brought over into the theatre or concert-room for this special purpose. It was also, by our standards, very small in numbers.

In trying to imagine what were the actual qualities of a performance under Bach or Handel, we have to remember above all things that the choir and the orchestra were roughly of equal size. This gives a totally different balance from that of modern practice. And within the orchestra itself there was a similar difference of proportion. The number of strings was small, the number of wind instruments by comparison large. Bach worked with about six violins, three or four violas, two 'cellos, and a bass, and was happy to have one good player in each part. Under Handel the oboes played in chorus like the strings, several players to one part, and even the trumpets might be similarly 'doubled'. The balance of the orchestra therefore, both internally and with respect to the chorus, was totally different from anything we normally encounter now. So marked is the change, that to our ears Handel's own performances would have been not only surprising, but probably very disagreeable. His whole force might be put on the platform of that Oxford music-room. At the first chord we should be distressed by the strident prominence of the wind instruments, which were not only numerous in proportion, but also very coarse in quality. And they rarely played in tune. That complaint is specifically made by many sensitive contemporary listeners. This failure was in great measure due to the instruments themselves. The accurate boring of a wood-wind instrument is a highly delicate task, and the result is never certain. Without an elaborate system of keys it is in fact impossible to make these instruments automatically true in pitch. The players therefore had to control irregular variations in pitch as best they could, and the discreet tone which a modern player learns to produce was quite unknown to the rough average of Handel's instrumentalists. We should be struck by the general reediness and coarseness of tone, and the longer we listened the more distressing it would become. The trumpets were in tune, but very prominent.

The violins were not enough, from our point of view, to give a firm string foundation to the full orchestra. The harpsichord, then an indispensable ingredient in all concerted music of orchestral type, was itself thin and metallic in tone, with a good deal of incisive brilliance, but no sustaining or expressive power. Add an organ when there was one, and against this ensemble the chorus was what we should consider hopelessly outnumbered. There is good reason to think that its tone too was predominantly reedy. Italian choir-boys still sing with what the Italians hold to be the natural tone of a child, a strong, clear, reedy treble. Human vocal chords are undoubtedly reeds in function, and the Italians justify their production on this ground. To them our more veiled falsetto-like treble is woolly and unnatural. *Chacun à son goût.* Yet the Sistine Choir to-day is probably much nearer to tradition than we are, and in the eighteenth century the whole of Europe accepted the vocal domination of Italy. It is in any case difficult to believe that anything but a strong reedy treble could have been heard at all. Handel's musicians, therefore, were this oddly assorted collection of singers and players, and the gradual evolution, from such beginnings, of our modern chorus and orchestra is an interesting story. Women first came substantially into the chorus in 1773, at the production of Thomas Arne's 'Judith'. That was the first great step.

Growth in size was certainly stimulated by the various Handel Commemorations, the first of which took place in Westminster Abbey in 1784, twenty-five years after his death. The various sections of performers in this event are worth study. There were fifty-nine sopranos,* forty-eight altos, eighty-three tenors (a number to make a modern conductor gasp!) and eighty-four basses, a total of two hundred and seventy-four singers. The orchestra numbered two hundred and fifty, plus an organ specially built at the west end of the nave! There were forty-eight first and forty-seven second violins, twenty-six violas, twenty-one 'cellos, fifteen double-basses, six flutes, twenty-six oboes, twenty-six bassoons, one double-bassoon, twelve trumpets, twelve horns, six trombones, four drums. The conductor, Mr. Joah Bates, played the organ. The solo singers are included in these figures; seven sopranos, one

* Eleven women, forty-seven boys, and one man. All the altos were men.

of them a man, three altos, all men, three tenors, and five basses. The chorus was thus not unlike a modern choral society in size, except for the overwhelming preponderance of men. The orchestra was twice as big as Wagner's utmost demands, four times as big as we should normally use for such purposes. The balance of the whole, and on such an occasion we may presume that the promoters exercised what seemed to them a proper care and selection, was from our point of view quite unmanageable. What did the chorus sound like as against ninety-five violins? And what impression could even these strings make on twenty-six oboes and twenty-six bassoons, not to mention twelve trumpets? Beethoven writes for two of each; Wagner at his grandest is content with four. It is true that the wind often doubled the voice-parts, but this only makes the chorus still more reedy and overpowered. We are faced with the unavoidable conclusion that performances of choral works in the eighteenth century were totally different, not only in degree, but in prevailing type of balance, from the standards of later times. There have been many Handel festivals since, and of much greater size. We have employed an orchestra of five hundred, but we put in nearly four thousand singers to make weight! This is much nearer to modern ideas of proportion.

Handel's own chorus and orchestra were in fact only roughly organized. They consisted of such musicians as could be conveniently assembled in a particular place, and as the players were multiplied, so more individuals were given to each part. We shall have to notice later the gradual adoption of more precise orchestral values. When they came, they for a long time virtually re-wrote Handel's scores. Mozart's additional accompaniments, which not only rearranged the orchestra but also added a great deal of new and more elaborate detail to Handel's broad harmonies, were devoted tributes to acknowledged masterpieces, but they destroyed the whole method of composition as Handel conceived it, and we have only lately begun to ask that these accretions should be banished and Handel's original ideas restored. We cannot go the whole way, for the harpsichord is obsolete and so is the broader musical relation between chorus and orchestra, but we can gain a good deal in clarity and directness of expression, and we can see more justly the essential features of Handel's style.

His music is particularly suited to players of average attainment. That is a very important consideration. The instrumental specialists had not then made orchestral parts so difficult that only exceptional players could play them at all. Within reasonable limits massed playing is effective by sheer numbers, and Handel is ideal for this purpose. And still more is this true of his voice parts. These are difficult by any standard, and if his long and elaborate passages had to be sung by a few voices only, a very high quality of execution would be necessary. It is remarkable that the very ablest singers have found Handel's arias suitable for their most advanced technique, while his chorus parts, hardly less difficult and exacting, have been the perennial delight of countless thousands of untrained voices. Given sufficient numbers, the limitations of the individual are lost in the massive brilliance of the crowd. And Handel was of course a singer's composer. He had spent his life among singers and these the best of his time. However great the apparent demands of his voice parts, they were always of strictly vocal quality,

and the more they were sung the more singable they
were felt to be.   They were parts one could live with,
year after year, good for the voice, good for the lungs,
thoroughly exhilarating as music, and incomparable as
a social recreation. A village choir might find them as
congenial as did the more sophisticated singers of a
metropolis, though in sober fact all singers, of whatever
quality, took to Handel as ducks take to water. He
needed no advertisement, no propaganda, no analytical
notes. The whole English musical world, and scores
of communities which had not hitherto produced
music on any considerable scale at all, accepted Handel
with a spontaneous fervour such as no other composer,
before or since, here or elsewhere, has ever evoked.

Needless to say, there have been detractors, particularly in circles which discuss music rather than make
it, and among those pseudo-advanced connoisseurs
who, like the poor, are always with us. Music as
popular as this, so felt the superior people, could not
possibly be of supreme quality. A universal taste must
invariably be a bad one. In the nineteenth century
some of these critics ran after Spohr, and Mendelssohn,
and Gounod, and many other idols of a day. Mendelssohn's own popularity soon disqualified him as a
prophet, and the rest had each but a short spell of
fashion. Handel swallowed them all. Indeed it was he
who indirectly gave the others such chances of a hearing
as they had. Nine out of ten choral societies were
formed to sing Handel. On his broad back they have
lived. Without him they would mostly never have existed.
They still in great part survive because Handel brings
them both their members and their public. Whether
we like it or not, there is no denying the fact that even
our Bach and our Brahms had in the first place to be

made possible by public support of 'The Messiah'. Naturally a conductor or soloist who had to perform this hardiest of annuals until it became almost a routine, might reasonably desire a change. He might even pray for a close season. But he soon discovered that a close season for Handel was too often a close season for the public also, and 'The Messiah' had to come back to pay the society's debts. Some people are no doubt genuinely shocked at the idea that an art of fine quality can yet pay its way. The fifth symphony of Beethoven is beginning to cause a certain misgiving to the aesthetes because it too, like 'The Messiah', has a way of filling the concert-hall. By present indications Bach's Mass in B minor may soon join these notorious best sellers. 'The Mass', as we are beginning to call it, seems destined to provide a livelihood for the more ambitious societies just as 'The Messiah' does for the humbler ones. And surely these are the real triumphs of music. It is precisely in the works by which all men can worship that an art most genuinely and profoundly lives. It is precisely this universal appeal of Handel which has brought him from the comparative privacy of a fashionable assembly-room into the democratic forum of teeming multitudes. Handel is everyman's composer, to a degree without parallel, and it would be sheer blindness to pretend that a repute so exceptional is not founded on exceptional genius.

Handel has both gained and suffered in repute by his general attitude to his art. He is detached, and without self-consciousness. He has no axe to grind. He is neither a reformer nor a preacher. He is not portraying his own state of mind, his own troubles and fears. He approaches his subject as an honest craftsman, ready to put into it the most fitting work and material he can devise for the purpose, but with no desire to write his own biography or cast over the work the shadows of his own moods. Matthew Arnold wrote of Shakespeare:

'Others abide our question. Thou art free.'

These words might well apply to Handel. We live with his music, and it is so spontaneous, direct, and healthy that we never pause to ask what manner of man he was, what buffets of fortune he had to endure, what struggles to win. He put himself completely into his subject, whatever it was, and forgot himself in a wide and generous humanity. His scale of values is that of average mankind. His religion is not the earnest analysis and intensity of Bach, but the normal man's sense of wonder and praise. His pathos is infinitely sympathetic, but never self-regarding. His heroism is a fine matter-of-fact courage, neither worried by doubts nor spoilt by vanity. He can be grand or gay, severe or trivial, careful or slap-dash. His vitality, his fertility, and his range of vision are as wide as his workmanship is apt and masterly. It is a remarkable tribute that when Handel shouts 'Hallelujah!' we cannot forbear to stand. It is a yet finer homage that in such moments no man thinks of Handel. We are carried away, as he was, by the patent sublimity of his theme.

3

Among the many artistic achievements of which the nineteenth century may legitimately boast, none is more remarkable than the organization and acceptance of the orchestra as a permanent musical instrument of the highest class. In what dim past men first began to find satisfaction in music without voices will never be known. The process was gradual, and must have depended as much on the persuasive power of the player as on the musical quality of the instrument. All early instruments are melodic, and in this first stage are imitators of the singing voice. Somewhere in history there is a great dividing line. On the farther side of it lies the slow transformation of the inflexions of speech into song, which gave melody its artistic form, but kept it still in close alliance with the character and range of speech. On the hither side arose that emancipated art which could enjoy the pure sounds as such, without either a verbal background or any direct appeal based on actual vocal utterance. It was the greatest of all the imaginative flights which music has achieved, and it is now so integral a part of our experience that we cannot easily realize how fundamental was the change. We still enjoy music without instruments, for that is the first and deepest of our intuitions, but our forefathers who learnt to appreciate music without voices were the real discoverers, opening up new artistic fields of which we cannot yet gauge the limits.

For a long time the old vocal associations were very strong, even in the case of instruments of inherently angular and unvocal quality. The easy notes of horn and trumpet are those of a bugle, suitable for an alarum or fanfare, but quite incapable of the smooth steps of vocal melody. Yet horn and trumpet, when first they were brought into the instrumental company, had to develop and practise those high and very difficult registers where their notes are closer together and can therefore play, like their orchestral companions, a vocal tune. So strong was this urge that players of the old 'natural' horn and trumpet had to master a technique which modern players find it hard to emulate. We have had to make a special Bach trumpet on which to play his elaborately melodic parts. Flute, oboe, and bassoon were always, within their respective ranges, capable of vocal melody. So were the whole family of bowed instruments. These latter were the only complete body of instruments having something like the sustained power and expressive quality of the voice. They were soon organized into a choir, though they are not quite homogeneous. The viola is too small for its compass, as compared with the violin, and its tone is therefore of another quality, but two violins, a viola, and a 'cello were near enough to the four main types of voice to be apt for vocal harmony. The double-bass is an extra. It belongs to the old viol family, and rarely had an independent part. It usually reinforced the 'cello part, in the same way as the pedals of an organ strengthen the bass.

This chorus of strings, several players to each part, was put into that space in front of the main stage which the Greeks called the Orchestra. That name was thus attached to the players also. Apart from the harpsichord, which gradually became superfluous except as a means by which the conductor could hold the orchestra together, all the other instruments were at first occasional, and used only for special effects. The cool quiet tone of the flute held ancient echoes of an hour's ease and intimacy. Oboes and bassoons were of the open air, suggesting rustic scenes and customs. They were in general estimation somewhat loud and raw, secular in feeling, and occasionally comic. The horn belonged to the huntsman, and recalled forests and wide spaces, distant calls and echoes. Trumpets were royal, or ceremonial, or martial, and they carried these weighty traditions with them. The appeal of all these instruments lay at first in precisely these varied powers of suggestion, and they were used dramatically to this end.

Massed together with the strings they formed a symphony, a general concourse of sounds. Thus came that
word into music, and it was ultimately narrowed down
to mean a particular form of extended orchestral music.
Sacred music did not stress these instrumental charac-
teristics quite so strongly as the theatre did, but they
were available for all purposes, with or without words.
Bach's wind, like Handel's, was used in the main
melodically, but specific effects of colour and suggestion
are found in both, Handel being perhaps more direct
and more dramatically minded in this respect than
Bach, though both were ready to underline a point of
instrumental association when needed.

All these instruments, thus loosely associated, came
into the private orchestras of great houses, and it was
there that orchestral music began to find its own specific
and independent forms. Here, as in so many other
spheres, there was much borrowing of ideas. Haydn's
early symphonies were called overtures, the theatre of
Italy having favoured an overture of several contrasted
movements arranged on a plan different from that of Lulli
and his followers, and nearer to the modern symphony.
Much was adapted from the suites of dances which had
been used for all kinds of instrumental music. The
minuet retained its place until Beethoven's time, and
movements of dance-like form and character persisted
long after they lost their professed titles. Many places
and many minds had a part in moulding these chamber
orchestras into the prevailing pattern which the nineteenth century has stereotyped, but by general consent
the most effective contribution was made by Joseph
Haydn, concert-master of the Princes Esterhazy from
1759 to 1790.

It is always tempting to dwell on the career and

character of Haydn, for no artist was more beloved, or
with better cause, by contemporaries and successors
alike. This choir-boy of St. Stephen's in Vienna was of
peasant stock, and he fortunately escaped the artificial
preservation of his voice. After many struggles and
uncertainties in early manhood he fell at last into the
cultivated household at Esterhazy, and there for thirty
years it was his business to provide music for as enlightened a patron as could then be found. So finely did
he control his Prince's band, so much and so masterly
was the music he wrote for it, that it may almost be said
that he made it a model for every subsequent orchestra
in the world. One or two instruments now common
were then occasional; the clarinet, with its great compass, its phenomenal power of *crescendo* and *diminuendo*,
and its strong contrasts of register, now piercing, now
hollow, now darkly mysterious; the trombones, most
powerful and solemn of all brass instruments; these
had yet to become permanent in their station. But no
new instrument has won an indispensable place in the
orchestra since Haydn died, and the hundred or more
symphonies he wrote are the foundations of orchestral
literature. When in due time symphonic music became the food of the musical public, these symphonies
were everywhere acclaimed. When this active interest
had its natural consequence in the building of concert
halls, Haydn's orchestra, like Handel's chorus, stamped
their size and form. By the beginning of the nineteenth
century these two provinces of concerted music were
virtually fixed in general design. Subsequent musical
history has been content to rest on these fundamental
plans.

Haydn's mature years fall into two sharp divisions,
those spent in the service of the Esterhazys, and those in

N

which he was free to live more publicly and to be hailed both in Vienna and abroad as the 'father' of the symphony and the most generally admired musician in Europe. With the Esterhazys he had an experience common to musicians in the eighteenth century, though rarely so congenial and fruitful as his. He and his players sometimes grew weary of their isolation, and even an ideal patron must sometimes appear to be a taskmaster. But just as Bach, by the very virtue of his comparatively narrow environment, had developed and expressed a unique and consistent musical character, so Haydn, in these thirty years of prescribed and steady work, evolved a method and a personality of wonderful fitness and constancy. He too was a craftsman of the first order. He wrote in a letter:

My Prince was always satisfied with my works; I not only had the encouragement of constant approval, but as conductor of an orchestra I could make experiments; . . . I was cut off from the world, there was no one to confuse or torment me, and I was forced to become original.'

Original he was, but with the originality of spontaneous sincerity. This is shown in his careful study of other men's work, in his unfailing acknowledgement of their merits, and in the way his own music reflects the frank honesty of his tastes and ideals. He was full of the folk-music of Croatia. He used and adapted these models, writing scores of warm human tunes with just that touch of the soil in them. And by inherent liveliness of thought and impeccable workmanship he built them into quartets and symphonies which are as fresh to-day as they were when he wrote them. He is said to have remarked that 'genius is always prolific'. He was ready to compose on any day, preferably in his best clothes, master of his craft, and at ease with the world.

His intercourse with Mozart is one of the pleasantest stories in artistic history. Mozart was both his pupil and his master; his pupil, when the young genius came to him for lessons and advice; his master, when in later years Haydn himself absorbed many things which Mozart had first discovered. Mozart died just about the time that Haydn, by the death of his Prince, found himself free to travel. The works by which we chiefly remember Haydn to-day, the twelve great symphonies and 'The Creation', were written in this later period. He was never too old to learn, and never too proud to admit himself a pupil. His last years were crowned by universal tributes of esteem. His two visits to London, and the symphonies he wrote for them, his equal welcome in Paris, his Oxford degree, above all the extraordinary consideration and regard shown him by the invading Napoleonic army which occupied Vienna; all these were proof of his hold on men's hearts. Still more were they proofs that European music had found a new horizon and was ready to appreciate it keenly. The orchestra had become an independent musical force, and hereafter its progress and triumphs were to be the supreme facts in the story of pure music.

Mozart died in 1791, Haydn in 1809, Beethoven in 1827, Schubert in 1828. Within a space of about fifty years the modern orchestra found its permanent form and its library of classical masterpieces. Mozart occupies a middle place in this development. He knew something of the earlier works of Haydn and his symphonies follow in the main the Haydn model. But Mozart had his own original and creative talent, and he was more sensitive to devices and subtleties of colour than any musician then living. The famous orchestra which had been trained by Stamitz at Mannheim impressed him greatly. Dr. Burney complains that even in this, the most disciplined orchestra of the time, the wind instruments were frequently out of tune, but Stamitz, and Cannabich his successor, had certainly trained their players to a precision and control of dynamic effect then most unusual. From this time orchestral scores begin to contain more than rough contrasts of tone. No doubt there was finely expressive playing long before there were expression marks, but in a company so varied and complex as the orchestra, less and less could be left to the momentary mood of the players, and more and more indications had to be given by the composer, as to quantities and qualities of tone production. Of this search for exact internal values Mozart was a product. When as a child he could distinguish and retain fractional differences of pitch between instruments in different places, when he fainted at his first hearing of a trumpet, these were evidences of a sensitiveness which was to find in the orchestra an ideal opportunity to show its unerring accuracy. Mozart's orchestra is of the eighteenth century, small in scale, but it is a delicately adjusted body of players in which all the details have an exact significance.

Mozart scored the Symphony in G minor for one flute, two oboes, two bassoons, and two horns, seven wind instruments in all; and the usual small body of strings. Within these modest bounds there was more orchestral magic than had yet been dreamed of. Each wind player is a soloist. That was the most important reform of Haydn and his contemporaries. The old rough chorus of oboes is gone. How far this was due to a conscious gain in sensitiveness, how much a restriction arising from the small numbers of a private orchestra, may be an open question. Whatever its cause, the change was of the utmost moment in the evolution of orchestral thought. The orchestra is not, perhaps fortunately, a logical instrument. It is the product of some centuries of varied trial and experience. It retains traces of that history, relics of circumstances and compromises now forgotten. The strings are still a chorus, as they were when instrumental music on a large scale was first attempted. It is this fact which enables us to adapt the symphonies of Haydn to modern conditions. We can, within reason, multiply the string players to suit our larger spaces. All the wind players, however, are soloists, and this gives us not only the beauties of individual tone-colours, each presented in clear purity, but it also gives us the direct and personal interpretations of individual players, a very important factor in orchestral effect. Mozart felt how a single sustained note on a wind instrument, projected against a background of strings, can be made to stand out like a star in the evening sky. The background is essential, and it can be infinitely expressive in itself, but against it can be placed all the individual colours and registers of the wind, each unique and separate, yet offering as many combinations as the imagination can desire. The wind instruments have never been accepted as complete families. Even when several related instruments are used, like the three varieties of oboe, soprano, alto (cor anglais), and bass (bassoon), they are used as individuals, not as masses. Later composers have of course used the orchestra unsparingly, including every massed effect of which it is capable, but every orchestrator of genius has sat at the feet of Mozart in this matter, learning the peculiar and specialized powers of each instrument, and well content if he could approach, with

however many resources and at however respectful
a distance, the unsurpassed quality which Mozart could
extract from a few notes perfectly poised.

The overtures, concertos, and symphonies of Mozart
are the finest flowers of the eighteenth century. Not
rarely they suggest a mood which was really beyond it.
Haydn was the last of the greater composers for whom
the patronage system of the old order was an accepted
and sufficient fact. It is significant that in Mozart's case
the system failed. Brilliant and successful as he was as
a child, and with many later triumphs hardly less complete, he yet never succeeded in finding a congenial
resting-place. The autocrat of his birth-place, the
Archbishop of Salzburg, who by the custom of the time
exercised almost an automatic right over the movements
and fortunes of his subjects, was of too mundane a
texture to appreciate the genius of his most gifted
servant. He provided neither opportunities nor encouragement. An artist without a patron was a ship
without anchor. Had Mozart lived longer, it is possible
that he might have found a better haven, though the
whole social fabric of the century was soon to be dissolved. As it was, his mature life was a series of restless
excursions, of momentary successes, of risk and uncertainty and neglect, and he died a comparative failure.
Everything is bought at a price, and the tenderness and
depth of pathos, on the verge of which even his lightest
pages will hover, reaches at times an intensity only the
more moving by its combined poignancy and restraint.
These are the qualities by which Mozart seems to
reflect his actual fate, that in the most musical society
in Europe the most sensitive artist of them all could
find no certain harbour.

4

Beethoven was a child of six when our American colonies declared their independence and roused the ardour of every democratic aspirant in the world. There is a curious link between Beethoven's boyhood and the American War of Independence. Some of the money which the English government paid for German mercenary troops, troops which were sent across the Atlantic and caused far more rebellious fury than they quelled, found its way into the coffers of the Elector of Cologne, in whose musical establishment at Bonn Beethoven's father and grandfather had been employed. The Elector spent some of this money, as was then the princely fashion, on productions of opera, and the young Beethoven's early education was thus indirectly fostered by these odd fruits of an English subsidy. The whole transaction has a grim irony. It is not often we subsidize the arts. This particular incident was perhaps an artistic gain, but it was certainly a political infamy. We neither achieved nor deserved success, and the world was rapidly becoming a place where civic struggles were infectious. The American example had no small effect on the French, and the French explosion of 1789 shook every vested interest in Europe. Beethoven moved to Vienna in 1792, at the age of twenty-two. A year later Louis XVI was executed, and the long turmoil began in which it was impossible for any active mind to be neutral. So long as the French peasants were fighting for their freedom every young and generous spirit was on their side. Napoleon the Consul, the hero of miraculous victories and to all appearances the very incarnation of popular liberties, was the idol not only of France, but of every party in Europe which sought to put an end to aristocratic domination and privilege. Napoleon's early campaigns would not have had their overwhelming success had not the peasants and reformers of other countries besides France felt that he was as much a deliverer as a conqueror. His gradual change of complexion, from the brilliant servant of the republic to the virtual autocrat of a new and insatiable empire, changed no less the hearts of many who had hitherto acclaimed him.

The varied nations and states of Europe, however determined to redress old abuses of their own, grew fierce in their opposition to a control which inflicted new and foreign tyrannies at the point of the French bayonet. Napoleon's assumption of the Crown was undoubtedly, to the ordinary mind, a clear betrayal of those public ideals for which France had ostensibly fought, and to which the populace of other nations, whether friendly or opposed in the open, had no less ardently adhered in their own several ways. The French taught Europe the arts of national enfranchisement and organization. She exhibited the strength of an emancipated people. With these same national weapons Europe ultimately defeated her, and dissolved the Napoleonic empire. But there was no return to the complacency of the past. Great reforms had been won, great redistributions of wealth and power, and the most conservative states were no longer proof against democratic ideas and methods. War and politics could not remain the squabbles of contending dynasties. They became the business of every citizen. The stage was set for those long and bitter struggles towards an expanding civil liberty which during the nineteenth century occupied a first place in the concern of every community in Europe.

The story of Beethoven's 'Eroica' Symphony is well

known. He planned it as a tribute to Napoleon, the hero of revolution and the guardian of liberty. When Napoleon accepted the status of Emperor, Beethoven was so enraged that he tore off the title-page and stamped on it in fury. This act of homage and its subsequent revocation was a symptom of the attitude adopted by all those who had democratic sympathies. In Beethoven's case it meant this and more. His family's livelihood, his traditions, and the whole environment in which his art had hitherto been practised, had owed their very existence to a system of patronage inseparably bound to the old order, to the resources and privileges of an aristocracy still almost feudal in its assumptions. The enlightened patron could no doubt be marvellously instrumental for good. He could encourage a fine taste with all the force of an autocrat. But he was still an autocrat, he held the fate of his servants at his will, his pleasure was their law, and however generously and humanely he might use these powers, the world was beginning to feel that the system was inherently intolerable. It was arbitrary even when it bestowed clear benefits. When it failed it was irre-mediable. There was a rising consciousness of broader values, of an appeal to humanity as a whole to evolve a different and more resilient society, a society in which contrasts of talent and fortune would no doubt continue to exist, but in which effort and ability might meet with more direct and public reward, irrespective of the accidents of birth and title.

When Beethoven came to Vienna in 1792, his chief hope, like that of all his contemporaries, lay in the patronage of influential amateurs. No artist could then succeed without the approval of the great houses, but Beethoven's attitude both to them and to his art was tinged from the first with a force and independence of character which made him a clear portent of change. His position was indeed oddly compounded. All his success was due to the unusual discrimination and loyalty of a select society. His fellow musicians found him unaccountable by ordinary canons, and he made no attempt to placate them. The public as a whole, so far as it had any pronounced views, was somewhat bewildered by the emphasis and waywardness of his moods. Yet his real appeal was emphatically to a wider world than that of the few enlightened amateurs who were his main and constant material support. Princes and nobles might be his pupils, might subscribe to his concerts and to his publications, and might relieve him by gifts. They might even go so far, and this was for many years his main source of income, as to pension him permanently, asking for nothing in return but such artistic intercourse or such lines of dedication as he might choose to bestow. None of these things made the slightest difference to his brusque manners, his open defiance of other men's views, his aggressive independence of character, and his conscious and expressed superiority of talent and will. The most remarkable feature of Beethoven's life in Vienna is not so much his own incomparable genius, as the faith and long sufferance of those friends and patrons whom no clumsiness of bearing, no fierce assertion of personal claims, however deliberate or exaggerated, could alienate. He might pass in a moment from friendliness to fury, without any excuse that ordinary people could find sufficient. His noble friends stood by him, whatever they thought of his whims, or of the general dissolution of social relations of which he was so formidable a sample. He could provide music of an originality and intensity beyond anything these friends had known, and so deep was their appreciation of the art that the vagaries of the artist were as nothing in the balance. Let him play and compose for them, and he might behave as he pleased. They were content.

And the music itself was as forcible as the author of it. Nothing so direct and vehement in expression had ever been heard before. This was no serenely ornamented talent, restrained in method and carefully poised in mood. Beethoven struck straight from the shoulder, and with an energy that shook the art to its foundations. Weber, after hearing the seventh symphony, said Beethoven was ready for the madhouse; and Weber was one of the most sensitive and gifted of musicians, with a strong bias in favour of musical and dramatic candour. Beethoven went too far, for him. We, to whom the symphonies of Beethoven are as the bread and butter of our artistic experience, can have little conception of the shock they gave to the ideals of the eighteenth century. His melodies were broad sweeps of concentrated emotion, his rhythms the insistent beat of elemental passions, his architecture the vast and varied panorama of all human experience. He was tragic and ironic in the same breath, first melting to tears and then laughing at himself, capable of ethereal beauty, yet equally capable of pages of wild rhetoric. So his contemporaries felt, and so we should feel towards some of the works which are now allowed to slumber, but which then were closely identified with his public repute. In the greater creations by which he is now almost exclusively known, he spared neither himself nor his interpreters. His vision was of the infinite, and more nearly than any other composer in history, he encompassed it.

'Fate knocking at the door' in the fifth symphony
may be a crude and unwarranted simile, but such
stories are not invented about works of meagre significance. With volcanic energy Beethoven summoned man to
heed those spiritual and emotional fires which so burned
within him. His range was the whole world of human
response to aesthetic stimulus, and the whole world
eventually heard him. His nine symphonies consolidated the modern orchestra. They helped to build the
halls where we play them. They filled Europe with a
new army of listeners who knew little of the past, who
were drawn from every strata of society, but who agreed
in their consciousness that here was a music which
belonged to all, which expressed not only the refined
reactions of the sensitive, but also the inarticulate but
none the less deep intuitions of mankind in the mass.
Thousands of men whose first visit to a concert-hall was
due to the repute of Beethoven's symphonies, found
themselves possessed of a new artistic vision. They
learnt to appreciate not only his music, but all music.
They became the new and anonymous patrons of the art,
modest in means but immense in number and enthusiasm,
who provided the only possible alternative to the private
munificence of a society which was fast disappearing.

This discovery of the orchestra by the European
public is a striking fact. No words were offered by it,
no story, no external appeal of any kind. It was just
stark music, unfolding its own unique values in its own
untranslatable language. It had as little connexion with
mundane affairs as pure mathematics. It was less
concrete than the most elusive poetry. It was an
adventure of the spirit, expressed in transient vibrations
of sound, as fleeting and as variable as thought, as
intangible as a dream. If testimony is ever needed to

refute the common accusation of materialism in the expanding consciousness of the nineteenth century, the growth and influence of orchestral music might well be cited. Never have men devoted themselves in greater numbers and with more purity of intent to the pursuit of ideas and intuitions completely divorced from the material exigencies of life. Never has the temple of art had more lofty aims or more disinterested servants.

That Beethoven willed this wide acceptance of his work was apparent both in his scores and in his behaviour. As a conductor, and the specialist conductor was then beginning to be indispensable, Beethoven was wildly extravagant. He would gesticulate with frenzy in moments of intense urgency or during a full battery of sound. He would crouch under his desk to hush the players to a pianissimo. His scores are full of detailed indications of contrast and emphasis. He was acutely demonstrative as a performer, and he intended his directions to be obeyed, the product of his imagination to be flung with full force at his audience. His was no sequestered art, no delicate entertainment for tender ears. He was an orator in music, and an orator incandescent with zeal. As the tragedy of his deafness increased inexorably, he was less and less able to hear the actual sounds, more and more possessed by the imaginative interpretations of his own mind. There came a time when the orchestra could no longer follow him, when he and they were not hearing the same things. He had to be taken from the conductor's desk and the direction given to another. Later came the unforgettable scene when his friends made him turn round to see the applause he could no longer hear. The composer who had so marvellously opened the gates of music to untold multitudes of men, was himself shut out.

5

The expansion of a musical public brings many other factors in its train. The age of Beethoven brought into the concert-hall a romantic movement similar to that which visited the theatre. In addition to the wider horizon which affected all the arts and encouraged a more lively appreciation of nature, an interest in local scenes and loyalties, and a feeling for social and corporate emotions, there was in the orchestra itself a new fund of associations. Every novel means suggests fresh ingenuit:~s of illustration, and a composer of ready mind could find in the orchestra many vivid ways of connecting music with external ideas of all kinds. Beethoven's 'Pastoral' Symphony is a classic instance. That artistic veteran, the cuckoo, was again made to suggest rustic sights and sounds, by imitative notes on a clarinet, then a comparatively new instrument. All kinds of instruments had done this before, but the clarinet did it better. There are not many other natural sounds which can be exactly imitated, but a tolerable thunder was afforded by blurred basses and drums, and the tricks and acrobatics of certain instruments could suggest various kinds of movement, and thus reasonably justify a musical symbolism for wind and rain, fire and water, and the noise of leaves or waves. Some of these devices are of venerable age and wide application. Tinkling scales on a spinet have done duty for a storm, just as have the rolling pedals of an organ. Bach's postboy, Handel's hailstones, and Haydn's sinuous worm all bespeak this ingenious telling of a story in apt musical terms. Beethoven safeguarded himself, and admonished his successors, by stating that his pastoral effects were to be taken as 'more feeling than painting'. But he was not so scrupulous in his battle pieces, and a whole school of writers in the nineteenth century followed to the utmost the frankly graphic method.

Given words to say or sing, or scenes to act, music falls quite naturally into the position of commentator, and a mind suitably endowed can give this comment a close significance. It may be merely apt and otherwise undistinguished, or it may blaze out into creative art of the highest order. But when music is made to produce effects of this kind without any accompaniment of actual words or scenes, then the dangers and limitations of the method become formidable. The public must of course be a partner in the game, and large audiences inevitably contain listeners of every degree of sensitiveness. There will be many, for example, to whom pure music is a mystery, and who will therefore welcome any kind of external help in the solution of the puzzle. They want to know what the music means, and if no story is forthcoming they may invent one. This is where moonlight or raindrops or humming-bees may come in, even though the composer had no vestige of such notions in his mind. If the composer himself provides a clue or a title, that is a great gain. If he gives a complete synopsis, better still. There is then a peg on which to hang our thoughts until we begin to understand the music for its own sake. Many associations are part of everybody's experience and therefore common to composer and public alike. There is church music and theatre music, the dance, the march, and the bugle-call. Mendelssohn can write a 'Reformation' symphony by using a Lutheran hymn-tune, a 'Scotch' symphony by giving to a melody a characteristic 'snap'. There are Haydn's symphonic jokes, like the 'Clock' and the 'Surprise'. There is his conscious representation of 'Chaos'. It sounds very far from chaotic now, but the intent is there. Musical experience is constantly adding to these devices. It is part of the composer's craft to know them, if only in order to avoid them. To a public whose musical education is growing, every such trick is a help, every clear recognition of it a delight. And the same holds good of the aesthetic associations which music has assimilated, including all the indefinable touches which give a melody or a harmony its emotional mood.

The most logical of all the musicians who have sought to build a descriptive art on these associations and allusions was Berlioz, who was born at the beginning of the nineteenth century. He began by adding enormously to the size of the orchestra and thus providing a new range of colours. He often asked for nearly twice the usual number of instruments, and he demanded every accessory in proportion. He thought consistently in genuine and exact orchestral terms, and he set out to picture, in the most vivid orchestral tints, the outline of a real or poetic drama deliberately chosen for its active and descriptive features. He depicted, so he averred, the joys of heaven and the pains of hell, peace and war, love and hate, the characters of men and women, their adventures, their triumphs and defeats, the scenes they witnessed, almost the words they spoke, and all this with no resource other than the tones and colours of the orchestra. This was concert music of an altogether new order, and it remains something of an enigma to this day. The repute of Berlioz is puzzling. He was unique, and some would rank him with the greatest. Most critics have felt, however, that even if his ideas were sound, and this is by no means universally admitted, he had not the purely musical endowment necessary to support so wide and so intense a fabric of external thought.

Liszt was akin to Berlioz in some of his methods, though his instincts were much more orthodox. He tried to combine classical forms with poetic meanings. His more ambitious works are now rarely heard, but he created a great impression and his influence was felt by many later men. Broadly speaking, programme-music as such does not last. If it survives as pure music, then its external framework ceases to be important. That has happened to scores of movements written by the greater masters. If the external story is really essential in order to justify the form, then a later generation will probably find a still more vivid manner of suggestion, and the new devices will supersede the old. The repute of programme-music is therefore as a rule contemporary, and the composer who in recent years has used descriptive methods with the most consistent public success is Richard Strauss, who was born in 1862. His symphonic poems, as such works are now generally described, cover every kind of incident and impression, from a baby's bath to a philosophic creed. He is ready and subtle in devising associations, old and new, which are apt for his story, and he uses an enormous orchestra with unfailing skill. But his greatest asset is not of his making at all. His apparent advantage over Berlioz and Liszt is simply the accident of time. Strauss came after Wagner, not before him. That is his main endorsement. In spite of Wagner's oft-repeated fiat that his descriptive music should not be divorced from its stage setting, he was himself persuaded to perform extracts on various occasions, and we have since cultivated the habit still more. Indeed, next to the classical symphonies and concertos, extracts from Wagner are among the most accepted items in our concert programmes. Thus played, away from the stage, they become programme-music, and they are at once so graphic as commentary and so original as music that they are welcomed equally by those who seek a story and by those who would avoid one. They have also added a whole new chain of associations. To go from Wagner's 'Ride of the Valkyries' to Strauss's 'Ride through the air' ('Don Quixote') is in the concert-hall merely a change of personal method, it is not a change of aim. Wagner indeed has so infected the public with this desire for convincing illustrations that not only the realists like Strauss, but the romantics and impressionists too, have hastened to provide intriguing titles and stories, and even some composers who were temperamentally quite alien to such methods have been constrained to offer at least an intellectual enigma for the public to muse upon.

All this descriptive music made enormous demands on the orchestra, because the new thunder must ever try to beat the old. Realism is either stark or second-hand. The orchestra was also constantly in use for the more direct accompaniment of words and scenes, and an effect just convincingly applied in the theatre, or in a concert with voices, soon gained a separate currency of its own. The technique of instruments was exploited to the last degree, their possible combinations tried far beyond anything the classics had dreamed of, and the concert-orchestra became so skilled and so complicated that a whole new set of considerations began to arise and exert great influence. There were many works that only a few orchestras could play at all. Average classical size and proficiency was no longer enough. The public, learning to know its music well, began to know one orchestra from another. It began to ask not only what was to be played, but which orchestra would play it. The next step followed inevitably. The best orchestra in the world cannot play by itself. In a vast modern score there is often little if any musical sense in some of the separate parts. These are only the bricks and mortar. Somebody must have a plan of the building and put detail in its proper place. This is the function of the conductor. An incompetent conductor is a public nuisance. A gifted conductor can do much even with an indifferent orchestra. He can remarkably enhance the powers of a good one. Thus the enthusiastic listener was led to make a third request. He asked for such a work to be played by such an orchestra under such a conductor. So infectious is the glamour of a personality that he at length put these questions in reverse order. Under modern conditions of publicity the conductor may in fact become, in average opinion, more important than the players, more important than the work, more important even than the composer.

Plus ça change, plus c'est la même chose. We have to some extent forsaken the phenomenal performer, but we have pushed the conductor into his place. We marvel at the fantastic popularity of the unnatural soprano in the eighteenth century, of the prima donna in the nineteenth. Their whims and foibles, their preposterous antics and staggering fees seem ridiculous, from our new angle of vision. But many of them were highly gifted artists, often of fine power and character. The public was merely human. It put these singers into the radiance of limelight, and then proceeded to worship the idol it had itself made. We are still human. We have changed the direction of our affections, that is all. We put the conductor on his pedestal and make his

executive ability the central feature of our view. We
then identify him with the whole product, players and
composers included. We applaud Beethoven, the conductor bows. We applaud the orchestra, the conductor
bows again. The day may come when this odd ritual
will seem as strange to our descendants as Farinelli's
laurels seem to us.

And the ritual is by no means empty. A successful
conductor now wields most of the power which for-
merly belonged to the patrons of music. He practically
decides what shall reach the ear of the public, and his
presentation of a new work may completely decide its
present fate. He naturally prefers music which suits
his own gifts or encourages the virtuosity of his forces.
If he is distinguished by a particular method or temperament, he is expected to behave true to form in
everything he undertakes. Those classics which should
have permanent and well-known traditions of interpretation are not permitted to be thus lacking in spice
and enterprise. They can be forcibly distorted this way
and that, and it is not only the ignorant who gape. The
whole process is quite natural and largely unconscious.
The conductor has become a virtuoso and acts as one.
The orchestra is his instrument, no more and no less.

Increased size, marvellously skilled playing, and the
emergence of the star conductor are all consequences
of public appreciation. They separate the orchestra of
to-day from that of a century ago. They are effects
we might naturally infer from the expansive fashions of
the nineteenth century. Their influence on our actual
music, however, could hardly be so easily foreseen.
Men of acute sensitiveness to colour, for example, like
Debussy and Delius, found in the modern orchestra
new worlds of beauty and significance, as far removed

from the traditional values of the classics as they were from the descriptive realists. Given an equally original harmonic sense, they could produce a music not to be fitted into any former category, a music rather bewildering to the plain man, but having obvious elements of delicacy, and subtle tinges of mood, which left a captivating echo in the listening ear. Only perfect playing and leadership can produce these works adequately, because they depend on the utmost nicety of intonation and gradation. They therefore belong, for the present at least, to orchestras of high professional skill. This same discovery of the uncanny proficiency of orchestral technique was made by the intellectual experimenters as well. Orchestral players of the first rank can play literally anything, within the compass of their instruments, altogether irrespective of its internal sense as a part, or of its external relation to any other part. At the same time they can produce a tone so attractive in itself that the word discord seems to lose what little was left of its old meaning. There was thus no reason why composers should not, if they so wished, put into their scores any and every melodic, rhythmic, or harmonic novelty which their fancies could suggest or their brains concoct. The word impossible disappeared, and conductors were no more to be beaten by orchestral scores they could not think, than were the players by parts which neither they nor any one else could logically follow. Here the plain man began to give up the struggle. If these extraordinary noises told a story of some kind he was prepared to listen, or at least give the orchestra a cheer for its prowess. But as music the whole thing meant nothing to him. A full programme of such works was not to be borne. He stayed away.

Young talents naturally gazed wistfully through these

advanced portals and strove to deserve a welcome. A
budding composer no longer has to convince and hold
a patron, or persuade his friends to perform his works.
He must approach a conductor, who has the keys of the
castle. If new works look technically interesting there
are few conductors who will not from time to time
perform a few of them, once. First performances still
have a certain cachet. Nine out of ten such works will
never be repeated. Under present conditions a few new
works are played once, fewer still get a second chance,
and only an immediate and resounding success will put
them into the orchestral repertory. The competition of
the older and safer masters is overwhelming. As works
by unknown men are usually chosen for some element
of novelty, a first performance may even create more
prejudice than approval. Failure too often leads to a
still more novel attempt. The steady development of
a talent which is deep rather than ingenious is very
difficult to achieve. Many suggestions have been made
with a view to giving young artists a better and more
sustained hearing, but the modern orchestra is a very
expensive instrument, and there are strict limits to its
charity, however worthy the cause.

6

Beethoven's orchestra differed little from that of Haydn
and Mozart. Only in the Choral Symphony did he ask
for much more. His distinction was rather in intensity
of temperament, in range of contrast, in general emphasis. His works can well bear the multiplication of
numbers under modern conditions. The length and
inherent grandeur of his larger movements make them
very suited to large spaces and many hearers. All subsequent composers of note wrote works of symphonic

size. The symphony, in the nineteenth century, became almost as much the object of every composer's ambition as the opera had been in the eighteenth. The vast majority of these compositions were heard once and then forgotten, but some have survived. Schubert's two last symphonies have worn as well as Beethoven's. Schumann and Mendelssohn have not held their ground so firmly, but one or two are still fairly recurrent. The mantle of Beethoven passed in fact not to these men but to Wagner. The writing of post-Beethoven symphonic music is not a matter of following approved forms. It lies in a symphonic structure of mind, a power to build extended movements in which the architecture grows out of the material. It is epic rather than lyric, well-proportioned rather than decorative. Wagner had the faculty, and so had Brahms, though the two were poles apart in character.

Brahms is one of those composers who have stood somewhat aloof from contemporary opinions, but whom time has vindicated. He steadfastly refused to follow either Wagnerian drama or symphonic realism. He pursued a steady and unexciting course, gradually developing a character and a method which were in fact one artistic whole, but predominantly conservative in tendency. His originality was not on the surface, and he never tried either to force it or to theorize about it. He was already mature as a pianist and writer of chamber music when he first turned to the symphony. He was highly esteemed by a small public and still more by a few very sensitive musical minds, but those who called his first symphony 'number ten', alluding thus to the nine of Beethoven, were greatly outnumbered by those who found his restrained colours uninspiring and his general conservatism old-fashioned. It is a remarkable fact that the winnowing of time has at length put him far nearer to Beethoven, in European opinion, than any other symphonic composer. His works are not in the least like Beethoven, but they do show as it were a ripening and mellowing of the musical ideals for which the best Viennese culture stood. Brahms is the end of the golden age of Vienna. German to the core, steeped in the associations of the past, he is the final product of a long process of musical cultivation. His repute was for a long time greatly overshadowed by the Wagnerian cult. When he died, in 1897, the feeling of the young and ardent school was that he was perhaps a musician's musician, a master with much lovely music and an impeccable taste, but inclined to be academic, given to too precise a technique and too deliberate a restraint. He was not at all fashionable, and rather a trial to the advanced. It was even said that his orchestration was poor. He never made a luscious noise like Wagner, nor did he lash himself into any kind of rhetoric.

A generation has passed since his death, and the orchestral music of Brahms has marched slowly and securely into a first place in public esteem. It is a most hopeful phenomenon, for it seems to show that general opinion will in the long run, after it matters not how many vagaries, return to discover what is permanently worth while. The musical public has, by trial and error, passed through an exhaustive process of education and has at length reached Brahms. It has found out what to him was instinctive, that the ultimate criterion of music is music, and not any other artistic notion whatever, and that fashions in art are a delusion, the essential creative force being at all times above and beyond them. Brahms stood firm against the whole realistic and descriptive school. He was romantic, but with the restrained romance of song and poetry. Time has justified him. We no doubt change his emphasis and take liberties with his classic severity of outline, but his stature is now clear, and the wealth of pure music which he has added to our heritage has earned its reward.

The present repute of Brahms is a striking example of that powerful trend towards the past which is characteristic of our age in so many spheres. Chronologically, the twentieth century is moving backwards, not forwards. The proportion of contemporary work in our programmes has steadily diminished over a long period of years. A century ago music of every kind was mainly contemporary, the chief exception being Handel. It was not necessarily the best music, but it was mostly written by men actively and presently busy in the art. To-day it is taking great risks, outside a few specialist communities, to offer contemporary programmes on a large scale. Only a handful of works command an extensive public. The fact is that the high specialization of the orchestra has specialized the composer too, and has to varying degrees specialized the public. Among a multitude of listeners there are groups differing widely in training and outlook. Those who think an art must be progressive at all costs often identify progress with novelty rather than with intensity of thought, and as such temperaments are usually impatient and aggressive, they frequently make an immediate impression out of all proportion to their size. They advertise the latest fashion and for a while give it currency. Time after time have they been speedily engulfed by more permanent and less vociferous tastes, but nothing will cure them, for to them the apex of progress is always at hand. Rising young composers follow one another with bewildering rapidity, and each is hailed in turn as the sure hope of the future.

Yet the number of undisputed masterpieces appears hardly to grow at all. Contemporary music has become a byword for thin audiences and financial difficulty. Our vast public is insatiable. It demands ever more and more music. But it walks backwards. In respect of steadily increasing performances and solid public favour, the greatest composer of the twentieth century is John Sebastian Bach, who died in 1750. He brings real grist to the mill. Concerts devoted entirely to his works are of extraordinary frequency, and they are not confined to the large centres. He infects the provinces too.

The process is particularly clear with regard to choral works. Public choral singing began with Handel. Haydn's 'Creation' was an instant favourite when it came. More slowly the Requiem of Mozart gained its place. So, under more ambitious auspices, did the Choral Symphony of Beethoven and his Mass in D. Popular verdicts endorsed Mendelssohn, and to a less extent Spohr. Mendelssohn's 'Elijah', a real contribution to dramatic concert-music on a sacred theme, was simple and direct in expression. It has kept a place. Spohr, advanced in his day, is practically obsolete, his many imitators all forgotten. The secular cantatas of Berlioz and Schumann have their share in the concert-hall, and so have many operas and operatic excerpts. Dvořák made choral contributions of fine quality, and so did the solid English school represented by Parry and Stanford. But of acknowledged masterpieces of recent times, written for normal resources and accepted by general European opinion, there are precisely three: Brahms's German Requiem, Verdi's Manzoni Requiem,

and Elgar's 'Dream of Gerontius'. None of these moves
far from classical traditions. Delius's 'Mass of Life' and
Vaughan-Williams's 'Sea Symphony' are more daring,
but they are so specialized in technique that only a few
societies can master them. Meanwhile the spaces that
used to be filled by contemporary works are increasingly
given to the Bach Passions and Cantatas, the B minor
Mass, and rediscoveries of the less known works of
Handel. No specifically modern work of repute reaches
the mass of our singers, and it is no exaggeration to say
that our performing societies as a whole live on the past.
Some occasionally struggle with the present. All fear
the future.

The orchestral outlook is hardly less confused. Of
symphonies since Brahms there is one by César Franck,
one or two by Dvořák, a few by Tchaikovsky and the
Russians. These are accepted and can be tolerably
played by the classical orchestra. The symphonies of
Mahler, Elgar, Vaughan Williams, and Bax, and the
many other works of symphonic size by Delius, Holst,
and others, can only be played, however broad their
aim, by large and exceptionally competent organizations. They can never fill the needs of the hundred
societies which would ask for nothing better than a new
symphony, if they could reasonably hope to master it
and thus persuade their public to support it. One symphonic composer there is who may yet come to his own.
Sibelius, like Brahms, has been content to express a
unique personality in terms untouched by any of the
surrounding fashions which have had their several days.
He was born in 1865, and the major part of his work is
therefore done. It includes eight symphonies. These
are just beginning to filter into our programmes. It is
possible that they may, like those of Brahms, gradually

gain a public appreciation by sheer force of musical character. They certainly have all the appearances of a body of work so sincerely conceived and so strongly wrought that time can only enhance the merit that is in them. And they are mostly written for moderate resources. If we give Sibelius a few more creative years and adopt the Brahms time-table, then about 1960 his reward may come. He may then be ripe to join the accepted company of the past.

This rough division into the possible past and the impossible present applies equally to the suites, overtures, and extracts from opera and ballet which enrich the general orchestral field. The playing of contemporary music is confined to a few centres with unusual means, and even there it is a small proportion. We seem to live in an age which, so far as the general musical public is concerned, expresses itself in admiration of what is gone. Our own original contributions to the art are by comparison few in number and precarious in appeal. When we want a packed and delighted audience we offer, not the music we are writing to-day, but the six Brandenburg concertos of Bach. Our best executive artists are those who can play Bach convincingly. Our conductors search his volumes for rarities. Our editors republish, our composers rearrange him. If ever a history of music is written which shall tell us, not the chronological order of composers, but how particular styles and ideals have affected in turn our corporate minds and hearts, then the early years of the twentieth century will have to be linked in very real fashion with the music of Bach. That he lived two hundred years ago is a matter of comparatively antiquarian interest. That he stands so firmly in the public taste of to-day is very significant. From the most

THE CONCERT-HALL

accomplished to the humblest circles, wherever men care about serious music at all, Bach is a present favourite. Such a verdict provokes thought. Shall we yet go still further back in our search for music congenial to our desires, or will contemporary music return in due time to the broader channels of contemporary taste?

MEN AND MACHINES

MEN AND MACHINES

I

IN a room sealed from the world, covered from floor to ceiling with material which destroys all the helpful echoes and resonances of a music-room, a clock silently marking the seconds, or a stop-watch ready to inform and warn when needed, no smallest glamour of publicity, no audience, no murmur of approval, not even a cough or a fidget to relieve the tension, a prominent red bulb now dark, now flickering, now in full glow, the only link with outer humanity a few technical engineers who control mysterious appliances and silently pass in and out; these are the conditions under which thousands of musicians work to-day, at all times and in many places, making music for the million.

If the studio is recording for the gramophone, there will be many preliminary trials to get the best possible balance of tonal quality and quantity. The music must be played again and again to make sure that the details are right, and that it will fit into a prescribed number of seconds, with no serious risk of deviation in the stress of performance. Once or twice it will be recorded on a soft wax and immediately replayed by the machine. It is an uncanny experience to hear one's voice or one's instrument thus come back, its qualities magnified, its faults and mannerisms only too plain. The consonants are too emphatic or the vowels all alike. There is a high note which 'blasts'. The piano jars in the treble and is inaudible in the bass. The violin finds an unsuspected 'wolf', a note which buzzes oddly. The tone may be too cold or the tremolo too pronounced. Finally, when performers and engineers are agreed that the best possible compromise has been reached, the master-record is made, usually in duplicate, every one being acutely aware that an error now is beyond correction. If anything goes wrong, the whole process must begin again. It is not unusual for a single four-minute record to entail half a dozen performances, and an hour or more of trial and discussion.

In a broadcasting studio performers are spared the nervous repetitions of the gramophone session, but they may be conscious of a million listeners, some keen but ignorant, some mildly interested, some expert in the particular programme, and a very large residue for whom music is a social habit rather than an artistic recreation. No echo of this public mind reaches the performer as he works. There is nothing to tell him what are the reactions of his hearers. There is cold silence before he begins. There is even colder silence when he ends. The red light goes, that is all. He has done. It is an atmosphere the like of which has never before surrounded the practice of an art. Not the stoniest audience that was ever collected can compete with the frigid stillness of those padded walls. If art is a process of infection, a mutual approach of minds in tune with one another, the one receiving what the other would give, no more antiseptic device has ever been invented than the studio of a recording or broadcasting company. And if conditions of work and social circumstances are deeply graven on the arts of the past, then it becomes a matter of keen interest to forecast, if one can, what effect an environment so novel will have on the art subjected to it.

Long before the development of the phonograph, or the spread of broadcasting, music had become, for large sections of the public, an accepted custom rather than

an aesthetic experience. The restaurant orchestra plays
to a clattering of service and a noise of talk above which
only a fringe of music is heard. Men are gregarious, and
if there is a town within reach the countrymen will
flock to it. Arrived there, they want to spend a good
deal of time in public haunts. Some of them form clubs.
Most of them join the town dwellers in public eating-
places and public entertainments. To most people
silence is unwelcome, public silence depressing. Pleasant social intercourse needs a good deal of bustle and
noise. The music of a social function may be well done,
but that is not its main purpose. It is intended to stimulate movement and conversation, giving a pleasant
feeling of general activity and well-being. Hard-
headed caterers would not add a band to the menu if
its only aim was to encourage aesthetic contemplation.
We are meant to listen, but with the outer ear only. The
music is not offered for undivided attention. There
would be consternation if we preferred the orchestra to
the baked meats. Music is provided as a kind of social
amenity, like central heating and electric light. It is
the aural counterpart of cheerful decoration.

In thousands of houses the gramophone or the wire-
less set chirrups away for hours on end, accompanying
but not disturbing the busy round of household
activities. We take both with us into the fields and
woods, on rivers and lakes, to sea, to the trenches, to
the jungle or the North Pole. These machines and the
ubiquitous motor-car have made the loneliest places
tolerable for the group-mind. They have relieved man
of his dullest companion, himself. Larks and rippling
brooks may suit poets and philosophers. Ordinary
people want other company, and the music-machine is
a reminder or a substitute. It is a solace to the lonely,

and a welcome addition to all communities whose powers of mutual entertainment are limited. Even on the lowest plane of taste it arouses a certain selective appreciation, and if the instrument becomes a real artistic companion, it can have very high aesthetic and intellectual value.

Both gramophones and broadcasters were compelled at first to cater mainly for the popular taste, for music as a social condiment or as a light entertainment. Musicians as such looked askance at the industry, and with good reason. Reproduction was poor and the material reproduced mostly worthless. This, however, was only a beginning. Entertainment continues to be important, because it is the main source of income, but room was gradually found for better music, ever more skilfully reproduced, until the present point was reached. Practically the whole body of the classics can now be heard through one or other of these mechanical devices, without leaving the hearth. Reproduction is by no means the same thing as actual performance, not only because of a certain minimum of unavoidable distortion, but also because there is in the concert-room something more than the music itself. There are sights as well as sounds, and a present and pervading community of interest which puts a real concert on an altogether different plane from the most convincing reproduction of it. But as a means of getting to know music really well the gramophone is without a rival. Movements can be repeated in a few hours more times than ten years of concert-going would provide. Records can be lent and borrowed. There are now many small social circles devoted to the gramophone, whose members have an astonishing knowledge of music. They may know nearly all the available classical music there is, and they know it better than any but professed specialists could ever have known it in the past. Confronted with a new style, they can play the work again and again until it yields up whatever value it may have. Reputations can be greatly helped by the gramophone, both of particular performers and of specific works.

Broadcasting is not, from a purely musical point of view, so powerful a means of exact education. It can give explanatory comment, and can cover a much wider field than any collection of records, but its sounds are fleeting and cannot be reproduced at will. One very decided limitation affects gramophone and broadcasting alike. Any performance which has its characteristic quality in the directly personal and magnetic style of the performer may fail completely on reproduction by a machine. There are singers whose artistry is irresistible in the concert-hall, but whose timbre of voice or idiosyncrasy of interpretation is unpleasantly magnified or distorted by the machine. There are players who sound cold and academic in public, but whose purity of tone and phrasing is such that hardly anything is lost by reproduction. There is no doubt that the machines are making a very decided selection from among the artists available, and this selection is in many ways sound. A singer must have a voice, and know how to control it. Passion and declamation are not enough. A player must minimize all the roughnesses often inseparable from any but the masterly command of an instrument. A dashing manner and a fiery enthusiasm are not enough. These restrictions are admirable in certain respects, but they do definitely weight the scales in favour of a particular class of performer. A mechanized public may never be allowed to know anything of an artist who is potentially great, but whose method is by mechanical standards clearly imperfect.

Who to-day would buy a record of Beethoven's piano-playing on its merits? His clumsy fingers, unequal technique, blurred pedalling, and intense emphasis were at times obvious blemishes even to those who listened under the spell of his actual presence. Mechanically reproduced they would be patent faults and no more. Who would buy a Bach cantata or a Handel oratorio on its merits, as these were produced by Bach in his own church or by Handel in his theatre? Would there be a market for John Dowland singing his songs, or Corelli playing his sonatas, or Haydn conducting his symphonies? And if machines are to be the main instruments of the future, how are we ever to hear music which is not immediately satisfying, or which is imperfectly played? There is hardly an outstanding work in history which has not had to train both its performers and its audience by repeated hearings, often very defective at first, but gradually approaching a fuller understanding and a consequent and acquired certainty of performance. This is one of the most serious handicaps which dogs all new work of real distinction to-day. It cannot by its very nature command the care and attention which we devote without stint to the classics. Not one, not a dozen, hearings will bring to it the security of the older favourites.

We must face the fact, whatever its effect, that by present signs a success mainly supported either by the gramophone or by broadcasting will be predominantly a technical success, an ever better reproduction of ever higher standards of skill, and the music which can command this careful attention will have to be already competent and secure. A struggling artist, deeply creative and working with utter sincerity, but with unequal results, may never get anywhere near these

channels of public favour. A mechanism cannot afford
to see beyond the present immaturity. It cannot take
the will for the deed. It cannot, in short, replace all
those helpful communities and all those personal efforts
from which everything we call good in music has come.
A machine which published experiments would never
survive to record a masterpiece. And even the recording of masterpieces may have serious consequences.
A Chippendale table can be exactly reproduced in
thousands, but that is the end of the craft. Singularity,
rarity, the direct personal struggle with obstinate
material, the momentary compromises and sudden
flashes of mastery, all these are inherent in the making
of a work of art. And a man must learn his trade somewhere, and be given some minimum degree of support
and encouragement during his apprenticeship.

2

Music has always involved three components: the
creative impulse of the composer, the interpretative
help of the performer, and the understanding mind of
the listener. All three are essential, but the degree of
separation between them has varied greatly. In the
Middle Ages a monastic musician might be at one and
the same time composer, performer, and listener. He
might write for his own choir, in which he also sang,
and the choir itself was the only receptive element.
There was no audience. That extreme case has since
occurred frequently in the production of chamber
music, the composer himself playing a part, with no
listeners other than his performing colleagues. In
simple secular music composer and performer were
usually the same person, but there was also an appeal to
a detached body of listeners. This was the case with the

minstrels and troubadours. It might be equally true of a village piper or fiddler who extemporized as he played. This close relation between composition and performance has been so natural and so persistent a practice that there is hardly a composer in history who was not also a gifted performer. The handling of instruments has been the normal approach to music. This connexion between creative thought and practical performance exists even in a case like that of Berlioz, who could not play any instrument tolerably. He and Wagner, who was only a very moderate player, had yet the practical experience of conducting, and both were experts at the task of directly organizing, training, and controlling an orchestra. The orchestra was their instrument. The notion that a composer is a man who sits dreaming apart has no justification whatever in history. All the outstanding men have been highly skilled at some particular and practical side of the art. All have had to busy themselves substantially with the rough-and-tumble of preparation and performance. Specialization has now reached the point, however, that it is possible for music to be written by men who can neither give a tolerable version of it themselves nor afford practical advice to others. In extreme cases the thought may be so far away from the realities of performance that it ceases to be practical music at all, in any generally accepted sense of the term. The notes can be played, of course, if they exist on the instruments, but there is nothing to prevent the writer from wandering into a wilderness of ingenuities quite outside genuine aesthetic reality. The result may be not so much an art as an intellectual exercise.

As between the two main types of performer, which we may roughly describe as amateur and professional respectively, there was for a long time no impassable gulf. It is not a matter of pay or status, but of average proficiency. Dr. John Bull played the virginals better than Queen Elizabeth, but not so immeasurably better that the old Queen could not enjoy stumbling pleasantly after him. Handel played the harpsichord uncommonly well, but his Suites, which he often called Lessons, were not beyond the grasp of his amateur acquaintances. Even Beethoven, by whose time professional playing had reached a very high standard, could yet write long and serious compositions which were not altogether out of reach of the Archduke and his friends. Only in the nineteenth century has there arisen a large class of instrumental compositions which no ordinary amateur can hope to get near. The gulf between amateur and professional is now wide for two reasons. Composers consistently write up to the technical limits of their instruments. That is not a new fashion, but its consequences become more and more pronounced. Secondly, the public now insists on superfine performances of everything. Students spend their time juggling with the latest artifices of thought or technique, while audiences swallow ever more dexterous exhibitions of professional parlour-tricks. Yet the easiest Preludes of Bach are better music than the Fantasias of Liszt, and a competent performance of good music is presumably more satisfying to the genuinely musical than a superlative show of shallow cleverness.

Listeners, again, can be divided into two classes: those who have at least a little practical musicianship, and those who have none. The former have always been the sources of sound and permanent taste. Much of the best music in our heritage has owed its welcome to those who made some kind of attempt to decipher it

with their own hands and voices. Abstract listeners
have of course always existed, but they have either been
guided by their more practical friends or have gone
wandering into all kinds of blind alleys. We have seen,
as in the chequered fortunes of the stage, what happens
when the pure spectator has too decisive a voice in the
arts. Similar results occur in every case where there is
no effective leadership of informed opinion. Popularity
and professionalism indeed frequently go hand in hand,
in opera as in football. A watching public prefers star
performers, be they conductors or cricketers. Only
an active focusing of practical criticism can keep this
trend within reasonable bounds. No great art has ever
arisen amongst a public in which everybody looked on.

These distinctions apply all the more closely to
mechanical music because to the ordinary pressure of
public favour is added the material risks of a trade. A
gramophone company has no choice. It pays its way by
the sale of entertainment, of which an overwhelming
proportion must be such as comparatively unmusical
people will buy, and buy in large quantities. The more
definitely artistic and educational sides of the industry
must wait on these general profits. A symphony is very
expensive to produce, and its market is small. Within
this narrow field technical quality is everything. No one
will buy a faulty record if a better one is to be had. Few
will buy a new work unless it has already had substantial success or wide advertisement. The gramophone cannot subsidize aspiring composers. It has to
be very circumspect with regard to aspiring performers,
unless their skill is already of unusual quality. The
gramophone will consolidate a reputation already made,
and disseminate music already approved, but it cannot
do much more.

Competitive broadcasting, of which there is now a good deal in the world, is the old concert promoter under new conditions. Publicity is its life, and in some countries it is chiefly an elaborate form of advertisement. Under such conditions it exists for profit, direct or indirect, and music is only a means to that end. It may launch some excellent musical programmes, but they must have above all else a publicity value, and this means famous performers and accepted works. It cannot be creative in artistic purpose, except by accident. It must provide what the public likes. Even broadcasting with a monopoly of resources must be in the main a purveyor of entertainment. Its artistic and educational departments are open to constant criticism, because its audience is an unmanageable jumble of conflicting tastes, and it cannot be all things to all men at one and the same time. To many of its listeners it becomes a domestic equivalent for restaurant-music, and such patrons want nothing difficult to listen to. Dances, variety entertainment, and that nondescript form of pleasant performance known as light music, are the main ingredients of its fare.

Speakers on artistic or educational subjects have to be fluent and pithy. If their information is also solid, so much the better, but weighty subjects can only be entrusted to weighty names. Home-truths from the unknown would be fiercely challenged. The pressure to engage well-known personalities is overwhelming, even if speaking is not their congenial work. Listeners want to hear famous men. They also want to hear famous singers and players, and the broadcasting company thus comes into competition with other producers of music, and is driven just as hard as they are to provide performers of unquestioned eminence.

It is all perfectly natural and, so far as can be fore-seen, quite unavoidable. All promoters of public entertainment have to take the world as they find it, and not even a semi-autocratic broadcasting company can permanently withstand public opinion, be it right or wrong. It is remarkable that such companies already contrive to include so many fine features. There is fortunately a good deal of inertia even amongst the most philistine listeners, and the company can often, by the combined arts of tact and advertisement, make its patrons accept many things which they would other-wise have condemned unheard.

But if broadcasting has come to stay, and in some form or other that is certain, and if it is to be, like our British Corporation, a public monopoly, then there are broad questions of policy which are going to entail very important artistic consequences. Suppose that a rough compromise has been reached as between entertainment for all and serious music for those who want it, and suppose that an agreed proportion of time and money may be spent on what is considered best worth doing, then there are two ways of approaching the task. A broadcasting company can either provide its own music, or it can subsidize productions already in being. To some extent it may do both, but there must always be a bias in favour of its own organizations, if only because outside broadcasts are not continually available. If we accept the idea of a continuous programme, then it is clear that outside events will not fill it. Public concerts do not take place just when and where they are wanted, every day, and the task of co-ordinating them to suit the company's full time-table is impossible. There must be 'studio' musicians, engaged to give their whole time to the service, if only to fill in the gaps between major events outside. And if in any event the company has to employ a considerable body of performers at head-quarters, why should it not aspire to produce its own programmes completely? The provision of a full studio orchestra and chorus becomes a clear economy of means, and an immense saving in administration.

Then performers and organizers alike begin to discover that performing in a studio is not the same as performing under the direct eye of the public. There is a lack of warmth, of incentive, and of encouragement which makes many things harder to do. For some types of programme an audience has to be brought in from outside. One cannot crack jokes in cold silence. In any case, if fine performances of good music will attract an audience, why should it not be admitted? The playing will be the better for it, and so will the enjoyment of those who can be present. The obvious solution is for the whole organization to migrate to a concert-hall for its most important musical events. The company advertises, and it has the best advertising apparatus in the world, it sells tickets, engages the best performers, and in fact begins definitely to compete with existing organizations for the favour of the public. There is no help for it. If the company gave its tickets away, the competition would be merely so much the keener. It can command enormous resources, it can pay large salaries and maximum fees, and it can fetch soloists and conductors from the ends of the earth. If the box-office responds, that is a gain, but it is not essential. The company can launch, with hardly a thought of the expense, a concert to which a packed audience could not contribute half the cost. The company's income is secured elsewhere. The audience is not of great importance, financially. But it soon becomes far from negligible in other respects. Thin audiences would be taken to mean that the company's concerts were not good enough. Repute and prestige as an artistic enterprise are involved, and the company, whether it will or no, begins to be judged by the amount of direct public patronage it can attract. It becomes a competing impresario, like any other promoter of public music, and is appraised as such.

It must do as others do. Festivals and other substantial organizations occasionally produce new and elaborate works. The company must do the same, only more regardless of cost. These events are a kind of musical poster, set out with every device of bold lines and colours, that no man may fail to appreciate their enterprising value. Other societies give first performances, and the company will lose caste if it lags behind them. Other societies take formidable risks. The company must out-bid them, and can do so without fear. It can spend large sums on the special production of works which no ordinary listener can begin to comprehend, works demanded by an advanced section, perhaps. It can safely perform novelties which even the warmest adherents of the future are content to hear once, and once only, and which no one else would ever want to hear at all. Though there may be a dozen better conductors or singers at home, it may engage foreign artists, at the equivalent of a dozen native fees, because the public still loves an imposing name, and the company's prestige is to this extent at stake. It is driven, in short, to all the well-worn devices which have been used and abused everywhere since public music began. The only substantial change lies in the fact that a powerful company cannot easily be bankrupt.

With regard to the subsidies given to outside enterprises, the same causes weight the scales in favour of those organizations which already have a high repute. An opera subsidy may go, not to the struggling native talent, but to such fashionable importations as offer a resounding artistic advertisement. From time to time a hearing may be given to more modest outside forces, both in theatre and concert. Even amateur or small societies may occasionally be given a broadcast, but these concessions are a favour, almost a condescension, on the company's part. It is not lack of goodwill. It is simply a question of technical standard. No public enterprise of so universal a nature can make its prevailing policy suit what public opinion would judge to be second-rate. Under conditions of modern publicity the company, if it competes at all, is inexorably driven to look for technical perfection, special accomplishment, general public repute. All the accepted fashions of concert-giving have to be followed, and the company succeeds in this sphere by virtue of superior resources, not by any essentially creative addition to the boundaries of the art.

If we begin to look for what broadcasting has done in the way of real contributions to musical experience, there is no doubt that most of these have come from its own studios, and from the occasional broadcasts of societies outside which cultivate a special province of music. The admirable series of Bach Cantatas, the Foundations of Music, and many other items old and new have been given by our British Corporation under ideal conditions in the studio, conditions of time and order, for instance, which no public concert could possibly adopt. And these things can be done by artists chosen solely for their competence, not for their advertising value. Opera can be tapped when it is available, and so can any interesting novelty or revival which an independent organization may have prepared. And there are plenty of public concerts of the usual type to be used, when such use is convenient. By these two activities, its own studios and its help to other efforts outside, a broadcasting company could make great contributions to the general musical enlightenment of the public, without in any way stifling or outbidding those who work for the art under ordinary conditions and risks. If the unique place which broadcasting must surely have in music is to be genuinely fruitful, it must either cease to be a monopoly, or else use that monopoly for the practical encouragement of all forms of artistic effort and taste. Otherwise we may in the end be reduced to a few well-equipped centres under broadcast control, fully justified by their quality of performance, but leaving little or no room for the more tentative and more creative sides of the art.

Singers and players might then be better, but they will certainly be fewer. Conductors will be extraordinarily competent and powerful, but they will have to hold their places by general efficiency rather than by the deeper artistic instincts. Even the occasional connexion between broadcasting and musical publication cannot do much for works of real originality. Masterly idioms are not the food of the music-shops, and a work's intrinsic sincerity and distinction are no measure of its present sale. Listeners will be more than ever disposed to forsake the amateur, either at home or in the concert-hall, and listen to the more accomplished fare provided for next to nothing. We may have to face, in sober fact, a change in the sources and circumstances of music as great as any that has yet occurred in history. These changes will make equivalent alterations in the character of the art. The general appreciation of music may grow stronger and more exact than ever before, the performance of it more skilful, but both these forces will live in the main on what the past has already created. The future, if it is to provide its own creative art, will need places to germinate in, to make trial and error, to feel its way toward its own forms of expression. The provision of this opportunity is the most difficult and most important task of our time.

Musical progress, in the long run, begins with musical composition; it ends when that impulse ceases. There would have been no Bach or Haydn without the countless contemporary composers who were equally busy and equally prolific. There would have been no Beethoven without his forgotten rivals, no Wagner without the many other operatic enterprises and fashions, good, bad, and indifferent. Germany has written and produced more dull and undistinguished symphonies than all the rest of the world put together. On that background she wrote the great ones. Art is not a sporadic growth. It is not a sudden or occasional opportunity. It is a habit of life, a creative impulse long implanted, and long nurtured.

3

At the present time England could advance impressive claims to be considered, in many important respects, the most musical nation in the world. We have no aristocratic traditions, no subsidies, and apart from broadcasting no State or semi-State enterprises which select, train, and employ our artists. Such music as we have is therefore spontaneous. We have no long lines of famous composers, no legacies of special patronage, no outstanding chains of executive performers passing

down an accepted tradition from master to pupil. We
have learnt to support a very great deal of music without
these aids, and we glean it where we will. London is
certainly more comprehensive in its taste than any other
city in the world. Berlin, Paris, and Rome cover more
of their own ground, but we, apart from opera, cover
the ground of all of them, and some of our own as well.
Nowhere is it possible to hear so many varieties of
music, old and new, native and foreign, as can be heard
in a London season. The Queen's Hall Promenade
Concerts have no rival in their inclusive programmes of
practically all the best orchestral music that exists.
Our choral societies perform every work, of every school,
which can be adapted to their resources, and of most
of the big works of the past they probably give more
performances than half Europe put together. Programmes which even in Germany are considered special
events can be produced and accepted here without
causing any unusual remark. We are catholic in taste
and reasonably efficient in performance, and though a
few foreign organizations can do certain things better
than we can, no such organization does so many
different things so well.

This general competence and wide appreciation is of
course subject to the reservation that we have no opera,
as Europe understands the term, and this may account
for the fact that Europe thinks we have no music.
Actually our springs go far deeper even than the impressive array of our festivals and larger concerts.
Wherever the team-spirit can be evoked, we make
music as naturally as we talk. Our choral societies are
teams, and this is why we have so many of them. Our
choirs and amateur orchestras are as spontaneous as our
clubs and committees. These essentially corporate and

democratic associations are a counterpart of our
political and industrial habits of life. Within these
limits we are second to none. Our schoolboys sing
cantatas and oratorios, and even produce occasionally
what in the larger world is called Grand Opera. It is
not too grand for keen youngsters in capable hands.
Our colliers play Wagner. They do it on brass instruments, the only ones that a horny hand can master in its
spare time. That is why brass instruments are popular.
No one can dig all day and have fingers fit for any other
instrument. These brass bands produce astonishing
results. They are often, in their sphere, hardly less
technically efficient than a good orchestra. It is open-
air music, suited to an open-air people, but it starts
thousands of men on a fine musical pilgrimage. They
would scorn the title of artist. There is no introspection
about them. They have discovered this brass band for
themselves. It is as frank and natural an expression of
character as their dissenting Chapel or their trade
lodge.

Provincial and suburban choirs, and they are legion,
sing 'The Messiah', in whole or in part. But some of
them are not unduly frightened by the B minor Mass,
a work admitted to be very hard indeed both to sing and
to interpret. We probably sing it as often as the rest of
the world all told. We have no subsidized orchestras,
apart from a few municipal enterprises in holiday
resorts, but we have an enormous body of amateur
players who join together, struggle away at the great
symphonies, and subsidize themselves. Let it be said
again, we have no Grand Opera, or only precariously
and occasionally. But the real reason for this lack is
rarely understood. The fact is that we do not take with
becoming seriousness those curious heroes and heroines

who express incredible emotions in foreign or incomprehensible words. Such paroxysms may suit other peoples well enough. They may feel like that. We do not, and when our friends try to impersonate these odd figures of grand opera we feel that something has gone wrong. A native and natural human being whom we know quite well has become an artificial stage puppet, vainly imitating, not what any person of our normal world could conceivably feel, but what an imported school of operatic deportment considers to be the proper antics and attitudes. The whole tradition comes from elsewhere, and we cannot swallow it. That is why such grand opera as we have has to be forcibly fed. It does not begin at home. We are not unmusical and we do any number of operas and operatic extracts in the concert-room, but when we put them on the stage, we are always trying to imitate an essentially exotic method, both in words, gestures, and situations. When the Germans produce 'Rigoletto', it becomes German. When the Italians perform Wagner, they Italianize him. But both nations have their own native repertory, and five productions out of six are taken from it. It is these native operas which have trained a spontaneous, and to them a natural, technique. We as yet have none, or so we think.

Yet when we leave the Wartburg and turn to the House of Lords, when we can find characters we can comprehend, words we can follow, and music which fits them, then any little town can produce opera, producers, conductors, singers, players, scene-painters, and the whole paraphernalia of the stage. Romantic knights and ladies are not of our acquaintances, nor are passionate villains or mythical gods. But yeomen and sentries maids at school and men on juries, lawyers and chan-

cellors, sailors and policemen, politicians and duchesses,
these we do understand. We can act them or caricature
them with complete conviction, and our friends will flock
to see us do it. Gilbert's plays and Sullivan's music will
fill our theatre or our improvised Corn Exchange for
nights on end. We possess more spontaneous amateur
opera than we can count. It is not the opera of Paris or
Vienna, but it is a far more genuine reflection of the tastes
and recreations of the modern workaday world. It is not
the elaborate convention of a professional tradition and a
wealthy patronage, but the natural product of average
talent, average leisure, the willing help of a community
of equals, and the consequent ability to make a very few
hints and a very few pounds go a long way. That our
prouder looks are still fixed on London and the greater
festivals, when they do not peer still farther and across
the Channel, makes no difference to these true arts of
the community. Naturally Queen's Hall and Covent
Garden are in another and a different world. The
suburbs and provinces make no attempt to compete
with them. They do in fact provide the audiences for
these larger events, but their own music has other aims.
It is something they do themselves, not a distant admiration of select specialists.

Last, but by no means least, there are the larger
churches and chapels, from which nearly all our past
leaders have come, as from their own churches came
also so many of the great foreign masters. These
permanent centres of a local and communal music still
go on, producing much undistinguished fare, but also
much of solid worth. Their choirs master the Oratorios
and Passions, their organists often keep a whole
neighbourhood in fine musical activity. Scores of
our most enterprising minds first learnt their musical

alphabet in such surroundings. And when all is done
and said, Bach's church of St. Thomas at Leipzig was
a far better school than Hasse's Opera at Dresden.

There is, however, one fundamental difference between these efforts of ours to-day and the not altogether
dissimilar impulses which helped Germany and Italy
towards their days of ascendancy. The Italian churches
and conservatorii were not only schools of players and
singers, they were schools of composition too. So were
the German churches, the houses of the nobles, and the
various musical associations of citizens. They played
and sang, but they also wrote music, and in prodigious
quantities. To-day the cheap reprinting of music makes
it very difficult for new works to compete with the overwhelming mass of the past. And it is not the rank and
file of the past which the modern composer has to con-
tend with. It is a selection of the very best which a
thousand years have been able to produce. No one can
live on composition now, except by a rare and lucky
stroke, and those who might add this craft to the
occupations of performing and teaching have no
obvious or immediate sphere in which they can employ
a creative talent practically. Perhaps the nearest
parallel is the present position of the painter, and of the
fine arts as a whole.

We all like to have pictures in our houses, but how
many of us buy anything which employs a living artist?
Our walls are covered with reproductions of old masterpieces. Modern painting must either attract the attention of the very few who have the means to buy, or
vanish as a professional art. It must in addition
consciously strive to differ from the past. Only by this
difference can it normally secure notice at all. Pictures
painted in classical styles are no longer saleable, not

because we do not admire them, but because all that is best in these styles has been reproduced by the million. So far has this process gone that buying pictures is, to the vast majority of men, a mere process of selection among thousands of reproductions. It would never occur to us, nor could we buy much if it did, to go to the studio of a living painter and look for a picture we should like to live with. Still less could we presume to commission a young artist to furnish our house with such decorative material as he and we together might think most suitable. Quite apart from the lack of means, it never enters our heads. We have homes in myriads, but no living artists working in them. The palaces of the past were fewer, but they found contemporary craftsmen and employed them. And if we were to spend on the arts of to-day a tithe of the resources we lavish on preserving and extolling the past, native and foreign, we should produce a new Renaissance in one generation. We have talent in plenty, but no use for it.

This is exactly what has happened to the craft of writing music. There is no need to indulge in awed romance about the task itself. Most of the music we play was written by busy craftsmen, who wrote it fluently and consistently as part of their duty. We have selected those we find most generally able and have ignored the rest. From time to time we unearth or rediscover one of these hundreds of forgotten composers, and find to our surprise that the gap between him and his better-known contemporary is not so great as we expected. Most of the forms and fashions which we attach to the one or two outstanding men of a period were just as clearly to be seen in scores of their fellow composers. In music as in painting it is often a matter of fine scholarship to pronounce on the authorship of unsigned works, and blunders are very easy to make. Our notion that composition is a rare and mysterious talent is simply the effect of our own habits. We live on the past, and composers are therefore few, very experimental, and for the most part failures. There is no demand whatever for that competent and applied workmanship which furnished most of the music of former times, and which would be as plentiful now as then, if there was anything for it to do.

If brass bands and amateur orchestras, church choirs and operatic societies, had to provide their own original music, it would be forthcoming, now as in the past. Children in elementary schools can write melodies not noticeably inferior to those in their song-books. Our schools of music are full of students who could provide any amount of sound and appropriate music, if their minds were set on the ordinary resources of our musical societies and if these societies could and would employ them. As it is, the craft of musical composition, like the craft of fine painting, is receding further and further from the normal mind and habit of our spreading civilization. A few individuals, by exceptional skill or fortune, succeed in attracting the patronage of a small and leisured section, but the mass of our people, be they never so busy developing their own hobbies and improving their own tastes, cannot come into direct touch with the many potentially creative minds of their own time. We employ a few outstanding architects on public enterprises, but our million houses are built to a pattern.

The natural and convincing reply to this argument, so far as music is concerned, is that it is clearly better to feed on Bach than on the undistinguished compositions of provincial organists. Here we get to the kernel of the problem, for Bach was in truth himself a provincial organist, and had not provincial organists at that time been composers as well, there would have been no Bach. Wagner, at the time his ideas were germinating, was a provincial conductor who, like his fellows, also wrote operas. Neither Bach nor Wagner, to take two contrasted types, could claim any peculiar status; they did what all their contemporaries were doing. Time has decided that they did it better than the others; that is their sole distinction. No candidate could approach a post such as Bach held without sound qualifications as a composer. The reason why our present-day organists and conductors are not writing music is simply the lack of demand. These men hold, between them, nearly all the most influential musical appointments. We have ceased to expect them to be creative as well. We ask them for high specialization of performance, and we get what we seek. Yet these are the only men in close touch with the mass of concerted singers and players, and they alone could supply in due quality and quantity a new musical repertory apt for present needs. A few specialist writers producing a few specialist works are no sufficient substitute. If our churches and concert-halls and opera-houses desired men who combined practical executive ability with a no less practical creative ability, they would find them, just as did the corporate patrons of music one or two centuries ago. The supply of potential genius does not fail. Nature is far too prodigal for that. What fails is the power of a society, mainly engrossed in reproducing the past, to provide for present arts and crafts. Had the eighteenth century behaved as we do, what should we know of it? What will our successors know of us?

There is not the slightest evidence that the funda-

mental impulses toward self-expression and corporate
ritual, which are the springs of all the arts, have suffered
any general diminution in the course of history.
They change their forms, and the phenomena of genius
are sometimes capricious, but the broad demand for
a measure of artistic experience is more widespread
than ever it was. The more certainly we provide food
and shelter, the more leisure have we to sing or enjoy a
song, to paint or buy a picture, to write or read a book.
We are immeasurably better off in all these material
respects than were some of the most gifted ages of the
past. Only those who know little that is accurate about
the Middle Ages, for example, can ignore the brutality
of serfdom and the stupor of extreme penury which
surrounded the very gates of palaces and castles
and cathedrals. A few select beings enjoyed resources
which were sometimes devoted to noble use. These
gave us some of our greatest artistic treasures. But of
enlightened freedom to develop a taste, such as our
present civilizations offer in ever-widening circles, no
medieval hovel had a trace. To think of music as an
almost universal hobby would have then seemed just
madness. We all know that even the best medieval
artisan would be overwhelmed with fear and wonder if
he could be brought back to watch one of our typical
mechanical processes. He would be no less transfixed
by the sight and sound of a cottage piano.

The artistic instinct is still alive, and the opportunities for its exercise are almost every man's portion to
some degree, and there can be little doubt that however
high the specialization of experts may become, there
will yet be in the aggregate a large number of people to
whom the arts are in the first place a personal and
practical concern. The machines will not kill them, any

more than the virtuosi did. They will escape notice, perhaps, and will have to live more and more on their own resources, but so long as direct artistic ideals and contacts bring a satisfaction denied to any passive appreciation, however intense, so long will there be men and women who make their own music. Some of the first problems of this activity are already solved. Voices were always to be had. Instruments are now nearly as easy to come by. The appreciation of music in the abstract is to all intents a conquered field. Even a tolerable practical proficiency is not difficult for those whose education is fortunate, or whose persistence is sufficiently strong. The last corner-stone of progress, that highest power and sensitiveness which results in the creation of new yet deeply grounded thoughts, which is not only consonant with tradition but also apt for its own time and purpose; this alone, on a scale commensurate with our broader means, remains to be brought to being.

For all we know or are likely to know, we may already be achieving this most desirable end. Here and there may exist young minds who for their own local players and for their own local singers are writing an apt music. We may hear little about them, and what little we do hear will seem of small importance. But their music may have, for all its narrow resource, the qualities which distinguish a fine art. It may have solid craftsmanship, and that will give it at least a chance of survival. Only a well-constructed art will stand wear and tear. It may express a consistent musical character, developed without strain and becoming ever more certain and commanding, not by virtue of conscious novelty, but by unassuming seriousness and sensitiveness of aim. This will give it a growing control of its own immediate surroundings. Finally, it may have in it the elements of so broad a humanity that every musical ear will find deep and lasting echoes in it. The rest lies with time and chance. Posterity may go another way, or it may turn to cherish this music. Known or unknown, such work may yet be not unworthy of the immortals.

INDEX OF PROPER NAMES